HUSBANDS!

HUSBANDS!

by

Patti Williams

LOGOS INTERNATIONAL
Plainfield, New Jersey

Scripture quotations are identified as follows:

KJV= King James version of the Holy Bible.
TLB= *The Living Bible: Paraphrased,*© 1971 by Tyndale House
   Publishers, Wheaton, Illinois 60187.

To my husband, Page,
"for better, for worse, for richer, for poorer,"
and to God,
whose love helped me understand these vows.

CONTENTS

Preface

After talking to hundreds of housewives, I have found that most of these women are basically unhappy with their lives. Over and over I have heard them say, as we discussed family life, "headship," "submission," and parenthood, "And what about me?"

In this book, I hope to challenge women readers with an answer to their question. I want to encourage them to accept their God-given role and not rebel against it. I also hope, by sharing my experiences, both in life and in counseling sessions, to help them develop a right mental attitude toward their responsibilities in family life which could prevent much unhappiness and unrest in their homes and in the world. I hope that women who read this book will come to realize that their main purpose is to

> Seek ye first the kingdom of God, and his righteousness; and all these things shall be added unto you (Matthew 6:33 KJV).

And to you who read this book, if there is one idea in it that will lift you up into the spiritual realm of the godly wife, then it will be worth all the toil, tears, and trust of those tried and triumphant truths lived out in the homes used as examples in these pages.

If there is something that helps you, then all I ask is that you *pass it on* in the name of our Lord Jesus Christ.

HUSBANDS

Chapter 1

What About Me?

So, here you sit at the kitchen table with another cup of coffee in your hand. The children have gone to school, and your husband left for work earlier than usual. You cannot understand why you feel so blue, and so down; worse yet, you even feel guilty about it.

You think to yourself, "If I had known marriage was going to be like this, I wouldn't have bothered." You have talked with your friends and they feel the same way you do—trapped, unloved, and on a merry-go-round.

Your husband stormed out of the house earlier than usual because he was mad at you for not responding to his desire for lovemaking when you woke up this morning. You spent the past hour trying to explain to him that you had been up with the baby all night, but he just wouldn't listen.

Your teenager was upset when he left for school because you weren't home when his teacher called yesterday to make an appointment with you to discuss his failing grade in science. He stormed out, shouting, "No one cares what happens to me."

Your younger son was upset last night because dad hadn't gotten home in time to take him to Little League, and the coach called and told little Tommy if he couldn't make it to practice, then he couldn't play in the game.

To top it off, one of the ladies in the choir came by and gave you a good lecture for not attending choir practice regularly. Knowing you would be moving in another month, you just sat there and let her complain and said nothing. You wonder what is going on and what to do.

Today, the family has turned from the "traditional family" into the "nuclear family." In the "traditional family," people lived together because they had to, and each one had many important jobs which made family life meaningful. Some of the main areas of activity were:

1. Procreation
2. Protection
3. Education
4. Recreation
5. Religious instruction
6. Status
7. Affection

In the nuclear family of today, all these unifying activities have greatly changed. Our nuclear families do not produce as many children since the population explosion and the pill. We have police forces and government protection; therefore, father doesn't have to protect the family as in years gone by. We have the school system to educate our children, and they no longer learn at mother's knee. The former family games have gone into an organized sports arena, and the religious teaching in the home is now almost always left to the church. The family is free to move all over the country, keeping family members separated instead of united as when grandma and grandpa lived within the same household or neighborhood as the children and grandchildren. The only thing the traditional family and the nuclear family have in common is their role in nurturing affection, mutual love.

In the traditional family, the girl was brought up to learn to cook, sew, keep house, tend to the smaller children, and thus become "trained" to be a housewife. The son was taught to work hard on the farm and do the chores, and to protect and educate the smaller children. Thus each was preparing for his or her roles later in life.

The nuclear family has nothing left in it to teach. We have educational systems of widely varying adequacy which do it for us. Therefore, when two young people come together in matrimony they are improperly and incompletely prepared to live the life set before them. This is why you feel unhappy, unloved, trapped—because you were not prepared for your role. Or worse yet, you don't even understand what your role is.

And just what is your role? First of all, accept the fact that you *are* married, and you are a woman. You made the decision to get married, now be adult enough to take the responsibilities that go with that decision. In Proverbs 31 we read what these responsibilities are:

> If you can find a truly good wife, she is worth more than precious gems! Her husband can trust her, and she will richly satisfy his needs. She will not hinder him, but help him all her life. She finds wool and flax and busily spins it. She buys imported foods, brought by ship from distant ports. She gets up before dawn to prepare breakfast for her household, and plans the day's work for her servant girls. She goes out to inspect a field, and buys it; with her own hands she plants a vineyard. She is energetic, a hard worker, and watches for bargains. She works far into the night!
>
> She sews for the poor, and generously gives to the needy. She has no fear of winter for her household, for she has made warm clothes for all of them. She also upholsters with finest tapestry; her own clothing is beautifully made—a purple gown of pure linen. Her husband is well known, for he sits in the council chamber

3

with the other civic leaders. She makes belted linen garments to sell to the merchants.

She is a woman of strength and dignity, and has no fear of old age. When she speaks, her words are wise, and kindness is the rule for everything she says. She watches carefully all that goes on throughout her household, and is never lazy. Her children stand and bless her; so does her husband. He praises her with these words: "There are many fine women in the world, but you are the best of them all!"

Charm can be deceptive and beauty doesn't last, but a woman who fears and reverences God shall be greatly praised. Praise her for the many fine things she does. These good deeds of hers shall bring her honor and recognition from even the leaders of the nations (Proverbs 31:10-31 TLB).

The following paragraphs express the key ideas in this passage:

"Truly good wife"—One who seeks God first and His will for her life. She knows God personally.

"Her husband can trust her"—Because of her identity with Christ, she will always be honest and truthful, always confront him with her views on family matters, and look first to her God and her husband for counsel and not to other men.

"She will not hinder him"—Behind every great man, there is very often an equally great woman. Be your husband's helpmeet.

"She buys bargains"—She does not exploit the family income by trying to impress the Joneses or by being selfish in her wants.

"She gets up before dawn"—She is organized, and by example, she teaches her husband and children to be organized.

"She is energetic"—She gets her strength from God and uses it to get important things done. She isn't lazy.

"She sews for the poor"—She is not selfish and knows the meaning of "love thy neighbor as thyself." She does not get all wrapped up in her own little family to the extent that she cannot see the needs of others.

"Her own clothing is beautifully made"—Because of her love for God and His orderliness, she is clean and attractive.

4

"Her husband is well-known"—Because of her love for God, she has accepted her role as a helpmeet and helps build up her husband so he will be known as the spiritual head of his wife and household, for if he cannot rule his own household, he cannot help rule in the council chambers.

"She is a woman of strength"—Because she seeks God first, her character is love, and she knows exactly what goes on in her household.

Because she is godly, her children and husband praise her. Her good deeds will bring her honor and recognition.

Now, are you ready to be that responsible?

You say, "But you don't know my family."

Of course, I don't know your family, but I suspect it is just like mine and, thus, this book can help you find happiness by sharing with you some divine viewpoints that have helped us.

Again I say, accept your role. You are a woman and you can't change that. You are also a wife, and you shouldn't be looking to change that either.

Women today are searching for happiness. They think, "If we could just get out of debt, if we could just buy that new home, if I could just have another baby, if I were just talented, if I just had a better husband, if I just had a husband, if my children were only older . . . On and on they wish, wish, wish. They are looking for happiness in an artificial society. They look for happiness in things, entertainment, escape, pills, alcohol, and worldly pleasures which are all counterfeits.

> What shall it profit a man, if he shall gain the whole world and lose his own soul? (Mark 8:36 KJV).

Yet God has already given women beauty, gentleness, love, a sensitive nature and understanding heart, intuition, and intelligence. The greatest happiness in all the world lies in the hands of a godly woman. We give birth to our children, and then have the responsibility to shape them and mold them. Our influence has no limit. Women will influence the world for generations to follow. Can't you accept this challenge? You hold the key to success or failure of your family. This is a tremendous responsibility, one that is God-given. In your very own home, you can change the world—but only if you are willing to be changed yourself. Change your mind, do away with your self-pity, and your worrying, and put your own wants and desires in perspective.

Sometimes women get so confused. It is easy to feel this way when the "weight of the world" rests on your shoulders, when you have to make all the decisions, be a wife, mother, chauffeur, housekeeper, bookkeeper, manager, so on and on. These things can depress you so much that you tend to go into self-pity.

"And what about me?" you ask.

Here is where maturity begins, the point when you become self-less instead of self-ish. True, you do often have grounds for complaint. But to whom can you complain? What is your role? Are you filling that role? If you are disgruntled with yourself and your home, begin to look at yourself. In Proverbs we read:

> Young [woman], do not resent it when God chastens and corrects you, for his punishment is proof of his love. Just as a father punishes a son he delights in to make him better, so the Lord corrects you (Proverbs 3:11-12 TLB).

Do you love yourself? Do you love your husband? Do you love your family? Love corrects, love disciplines, love shares, love protects, love is patient, love is kind. If you are the disgruntled one in your home, then you are the one to begin the change, and you do it by making a decision. You decide you do not want your marriage the way it is—then you make the decision to change and be mature enough to follow through with that decision. Begin now to see your family from God's viewpoint. Find out how He wants your household to operate.

It is only a mature woman who can withstand the pressures of life today and still be happy and content. You make the decision. Do you want to be a godly woman? First of all, you have to admit you are unhappy. You have to admit, "Maybe I don't love my husband," or "Maybe my husband doesn't love me." "Do I really want to know?"

"Do I care enough to change?" A woman has to be willing to be a helpmeet whatever the cost. She must be willing to come under her husband's rule, and to come under God's divine order in their relationship. He may be a scoundrel, but if she cares enough, she will help him, no matter what the cost. Unless of course she is selfish and only loves herself. Or if she rebels and doesn't want to help him or herself. Or she may just be tired and give out instead of giving up. You see, when you give up, you can surrender and call on God to guide you the rest of the way.

Chapter 2

What About Him?

I had a phone call the other day from a woman who needed counseling. As we talked on the phone, she moaned that her husband wasn't a Christian, and she wanted to know what she could do. She had been very unhappily married for fifteen years, but, she claimed, if her husband would only become a Christian, everything would be all right.

I asked, "Did you know your husband wasn't a Christian before you married him?"

"Well, I didn't ever ask," she grunted.

"Were you a Christian?"

"Oh, yes, I accepted Christ when I was eleven years old."

I told her she had already broken God's law by marrying someone who was not a Christian and that she had brought these problems on herself. She coughed a little and said, "Someone is at my door. I have to go now."

All these years, this lady blamed her husband because he wasn't a Christian, and yet she had not set the example or even attempted to do as Peter says:

> Wives, fit in with your husbands' plans; for then if they refuse to listen when you talk to them about the Lord, they will be won by your respectful, pure behavior. Your godly lives will speak to them better than any words (I Peter 3:1 TLB).

Now maybe you married your husband under the assumption that he was a Christian. Maybe when you met him he was singing in the church choir or teaching a Sunday School class at the local church, and he claimed to be a Christian. Great! But wait! Say, for example, you have been married fifteen years and over that time your relationship with God has been growing deeper and more meaningful, but your husband hasn't progressed along with you. You begin to feel that he doesn't love you. He seems to care more about impressing others with superficial things rather than impressing you with real growth in God.

> Don't be selfish; don't live to make a good impression on others. Be humble, thinking of others as better than yourself. (Philippians 2:3 TLB).

Question his salvation. If it will save your marriage, why not? I know one man who had a ready testimony of salvation, in which he accepted Christ as a twelve-year-old. He always said he didn't remember much about the decision, but he did remember his heart beat faster when he went up to shake the pastor's hand. For forty-five years he gave this testimony, yet his actions did not show a Christian love to his wife or family.

> Now your attitudes and thoughts must all be constantly changing for the better (Ephesians 4:23 TLB).

Oh, he was a good man, did all the things that nice, self-righteous men do, yet there was something lacking in his life. He was empty and frustrated. On one occasion he was having family problems and came for counseling. We questioned him intensely about his life. He told us that as a child he had experimented with sexual activities with other boys and had guilty feelings about it, yet, after accepting Christ (he thought), he still felt guilty, and all his life he has remained sexually perverted. This was one of his hang-ups with his wife and his relationship.

As we counseled him we helped him realize that in accepting Christ, all the guilt goes away and your life changes.

> Live no longer as the unsaved do, for they are blinded and confused. Their closed hearts are full of darkness; they are far away from the life of God because they have shut their minds against him, and they cannot understand his ways. They don't care anymore about right and wrong and have given themselves over to impure ways. They stop at nothing, being driven by their evil minds and reckless lusts (Ephesians 4:17-19 TLB).

Yet this man had not changed from his sexual perversion. Then he realized that he had never really trusted Jesus as his Savior. The Holy Spirit convicted his heart, we prayed with him, and in our living room, he accepted Christ as his Savior and Lord. In subsequent months, we were delighted to hear that he changed, his family life changed, and he and his wife are getting along beautifully in their new relationship.

All his life, this man was misled by depending on a "feeling" rather than on an actual event of having his sins forgiven and his spirit brought to life by God's power.

The most frustrated person is the one who claims that he knows God and really doesn't.

> Not all who sound religious are really godly people. They may refer to me as 'Lord', but still won't get to heaven. For the decisive question is whether they obey my Father in heaven. (Matthew 7:21 TLB).

So if you are grumbling about your husband not being a Christian, remember, it is you who made the decision to marry him. As a Christian, you should have found out before you married him what his relationship to God was.

Now that you are married, the time for grumbling is over. You need to apply your efforts to helping him become a full participator in the Christian life.

It is true that many men are turned off by their so-called Christian wives. In the next chapter, we will discuss some of the ways that husbands are turned off and tuned out.

Chapter 3

Turned Off and Tuned Out

"Where have you been, Lil?" asked Jim. "I have been home for a half hour, the kids are running around the neighborhood, and supper isn't even ready."

"Well, Jim, I've been to my prayer and sharing group, and it lasted longer than I thought it would," answered Lil, in hopes of making a good excuse.

"I sure hope you prayed for yourself to be a better mother and wife. This place is a mess. It's a wonder the state board of health hasn't been out here. You think more of that group than you do your own family," Jim went on, his voice smoldering. "All I ever hear is prayer group and all I ever see is a mess. I thought your God was a God of order. Well, you sure don't have any order around here. It is chaos. I am sick and tired of dirty diapers in the toilet, dirty dishes in the sink, and dirty sheets on the bed. I've had it with you and your religion."

"Honey, is anything wrong?" Lori asked Dick as he sat in the chair sulking.

"As a matter of fact, yes!" shouted Dick. "Today when we had that tornado watch, I called home and you weren't here. Judy answered the phone and said that you were at the church. Don't you have any love for your family—to leave our eight-year-old daughter in the house by herself during a tornado watch?"

"I'm sorry, but I was helping one of the girls who was having a problem at home."

"Well, who is more important, your own daughter, or some dumb woman gossiping about her family and dumping all her problems on you?" Dick retorted.

Many women are flitting here and there trying to find an answer to their emptiness—trying even in the realm of religion—and yet losing sight of their first and foremost responsibilities, as wives, and mothers.

One woman tried for years to convert her husband to Christ. She went to church and claimed to be Spirit-filled, but all the while she was secretly in love with the choir director, carrying on a fantasy affair. In her prayer group, she was quick to tell all the girls how to live their lives and to ask them to pray for her husband. She is the one who needed the prayer. No wonder her husband was turned off. She was giving to others the time and attention that rightfully belonged to him, and she was doing it in the name of religion.

I have seen many of the prayer groups and sharing sessions turn into havoc when feelings among the opposite sex are shared. I am not trying to be negative toward the sharing groups as such. The point is that some women are prone to use these as well as other church-related activities to sublimate their marital frustrations. Also, some men may take advantage of such women's instability, a situation similar to the one Paul is trying to warn Timothy about in the following Scripture:

> They are the kind who craftily sneak into other people's homes and make friendships with silly, sin-burdened women and teach

14

them their new doctrines. Women of that kind are forever following new teachers, but they never understand the truth. And these teachers fight truth just as Jannes and Jambres fought against Moses. They have dirty minds, warped and twisted, and have turned against the Christian faith (II Timothy 3:6-8 TLB).

Remember, Peter writes that husbands will be won by your respectful pure behavior. Your godly life will speak to your mate better than any words.

One of the things we women really seem to use is our tongue. We can cut a man down so quickly and tear him into shreds in no time. Of course, we are honest, but the Christian woman offers advice and honesty in love. Some women have a habit of offering advice in high-pitched fury.

"Why are you always tuned out?" Ann asked Joe.

"You call yourself Christian, and yet you have been ranting and raving all evening in front of the children. Little Sandy was so scared she crawled under the dining-room table to get out of the firing line. Can't you use your inside voice and quit shouting? In this family, we are all under thirty-five and not hard of hearing yet," stated Joe.

One mother related that her children weren't doing well in school because they weren't listening to the teacher who talked softly and sweetly. These children were used to hearing the loud voice of their mother and didn't respond to the teacher because she was so quiet. In fact, they didn't know how to respond unless someone shouted at them.

These are just a few things that turn our husbands off and cause them to tune us out.

We wives somewhere along the line have gotten a misconception of what Peter meant when he wrote:

> Likewise, ye wives, be in subjection to your own husbands; that, if any obey not the word, they also may without the word be won by the conversation of the wives (I Peter 3:1 KJV).

What's wrong is that we have not been fitting into our husband's plans. A Christian wife who has a husband who is out of divine order (and by this I mean letting Christ be his head and him being the head of his family), has the responsibility of winning him into divine order. She does this by willingly placing herself under her husband's authority in the prayerful attitude of a winsome personality and character. She places herself under her husband's government, right or wrong; when it is right, she helps keep it right, when wrong, she helps put it right. It is by her wholesome life that she will win her husband's respect. If she has the voice and manner of Christ, she will be winsome. She will display a personal magnetism which will evoke respect, beget affection, and win admiration for the name of Jesus Christ.

The point is, when a woman gets married, whether she is aware of it or not, she gives up her personal freedom for a greater freedom within the framework of the holy estate of matrimony. It is here that she exercises the freedom to become the right wife for her right husband and the two halves become one whole—they complete each other. She makes up his lacks, helps supply the missing qualities in his life, fulfills his needs, and he does the same for her. She fulfills his social as well as sexual needs, his public as well as private needs, his psychological as well as physiological needs, his spiritual as well as his emotional needs. They supplement each other and together achieve what neither of them could do alone.

Therefore, wives who are coming out from under the authority of their husbands for their own personal freedom are doing violence to the plan of God. They are not fitting into God's plan nor meeting the needs of their husbands. They literally abandon their husbands to an incomplete life, and refuse to help them become what they should be.

The office of wife and mother is not inferior nor superior to the office of husband and father—they are simply two different offices which are interdependent. However, in God's plan for order and freedom, He did ordain that man be the head of his wife. Wives who balk at this divine plan will find themselves on a walk—alone.

Coming under the authority of your husband does not mean complying with his every wish, demand, or command. It means to exercise your privilege as a wife and to supply him in the areas where he is deficient, correct him in the areas where he is wrong, and compliment him in the areas where he is right.

It is true that the man has a tremendous responsibility as head of the home, and he must bear the blame when the business of family life degenerates. But the role of the wife is also a great responsibility, for she is given the "impossible" task of moving an immovable object. Her man is often a mountain of frustrations, and she has the job of winning her husband to the Master by her unselfish devotion, by her loving acts and her tactfulness. She must be about her Father's business, and what an enterprise, what a challenge!

Why do some women find marriage so boring, so bad, so belittling? It is because they have gotten themselves in the wrong position—they have tried to center their marriage around themselves or their children. Put Christ at the center, put yourself lovingly under the authority of your husband, and the children under you and your husband's authority, and then watch your marriage come alive.

The motive for voluntarily submitting yourself to the authority of your husband is to win him to Jesus Christ and into divine order. What greater motive can there be? Contrary to what many people think, love is discipline, not indulgence. It is by your discipline, your purity, your prayers, your correct conduct that you influence and motivate your husband to be the spiritual leader of the home.

It seems a paradox that you put yourself under your husband's rule by honest confrontation and correction. But nonetheless, this is the way you do it. If you did not care, you would go your way (be liberated) and he his, and what kind of marriage would that be?

For example: If your husband asks you out to dinner one even-

17

ing, just the two of you alone in a nice fancy restaurant, what should be your response? It seems like a foregone conclusion that if you are coming under your husband's authority you would jump for joy, accept the invitation, and comply with his wishes. On the other hand, if you are really coming under your husband's authority, and you know from past experience that he never thinks ahead and he will be blowing the budget if you splurge and go out and eat, the loving response might well be the opposite one.

In this case, you would lovingly explain to your husband that the budget would not permit it, but it was a sweet thought. You will have to be the one to exercise self-discipline. Remember, one of the fruits of the Spirit is self-discipline, and if he is not a Christian, he will not always be aware of this biblical principle. Also, he is not protecting you, for should you decide to go anyway, you will have to answer the phone when the bill collector calls. Thus your husband's "kindness" has exposed you and hurt you.

Now some wives have a problem here, too, as they don't want the responsibility of having to teach their husband, or the responsibility of making the decision, or the responsibility of being self-disciplined. As one woman put it, "If I had wanted to be his mother I would have adopted him." I know how she felt, but I know, too, that by marrying our husbands we committed ourselves to help them, which may well put us in the role of teacher. It's all part of learning to reverence your husband as you do the Lord.

Chapter 4

Rebel Without a Cause

There are some wives who choose to use "religion" to compensate for their unhappiness. They go here and there searching for meaning in church activity and sharing groups. They seem to think this is more important than their family responsibilities. One woman said that I could use her testimony of how God had dealt with her in this matter:

I felt a void in my life. There seemed to be something missing. I saw my husband going off to his exciting job and playing golf with the guys every Sunday afternoon. He seemed to be getting such a kick out of life. My children were enjoying themselves—I did all the cooking, ironing, picking up of their rooms. Nobody seemed to appreciate what I was doing. I began to wallow in self-pity and to rebel. In order to rationalize my rebellion, I chose to get involved in every church activity I could find. My attitude was terrible. I decided to let each member of the family fend for himself while I went out to get a lot of praise and appreciation for the good works I was doing in the church.

I felt proud of my accomplishments. I was really building up the

Sunday school class I was teaching, and I felt I was the savior of the choir. But the more I participated in what I thought were good things, the more hassle it created at home. My husband would argue with me almost every night. This would make me angry. I would spend money like a maniac, creating bills we could not pay. I began sharing my personal problems with others. I would complain to others about how terrible my husband was. Before I knew it, I had become the joke of the town. When people wanted to gossip, I was the prime victim because of my own big mouth.

So when all these problems of home and church and finances began to pile up as I sought to fill the void in my life, I knew something had to be done. I was overwhelmed with problems and was full of self-pity, resentment, and bitterness.

One day I just gave up and said, "Okay, God, change me." In my prayers I told God exactly how I felt. I was angry with my family. I felt sorry for myself. I wanted my attitude to change.

God showed me that it was in putting Him first that I would overcome my problems, and the void in my life would be filled. I was beginning to be filled up with the Spirit of God through my daily prayer life. I began praying without ceasing as I drove in the car, at the kitchen sink, in bed at night, while waiting in the doctor's office, while shopping—everywhere and any time.

God did indeed take first place in my life, and as He did, my relationship with my husband and children took on the right perspective. It was not the church or the sharing groups or garden club or P. T. O.—it was my family. I realized that I had dissipated my energy in a flurry of religious activity. God revealed to me that I "used" the church and got burdened down with church activity in order to shirk my home responsibility. I now know that I "serve Him" by being a helpmeet to my husband and a better mother to my children through putting God first in my life and I no longer rebel against my role.

Many women try to handle their unhappiness by sharing their troubles with just anyone. This can get them into serious trouble. If you share with another man, you could eventually become involved and blow the whole bit. Others share with their friends, and this makes the friends begin to feel hostile towards the husband, thus breaking up friendships.

20

It is not always wise to share with your parents, because should you and your husband be reconciled, it is easy for you to forgive him, but your sympathetic parents will still hold those grievances against him, thus making the family miserable.

Sharing is a way of witnessing—but when a wife shares her family frustrations with her parents she may find herself with a problem. One lady told me of her experience along this line. She and her husband were having all kinds of problems in adjusting; emotional immaturity, discipline of children, sex, finances. She relayed all the details to her mother, who in turn passed them along to the father. Finally, the couple decided to separate. She then went back home and really vented her bitterness and resentment of her husband to her parents.

However, as is so often the case, as time went by the wife and husband realized their mistakes and immaturity and they happily reunited. Unfortunately, the wife's parents couldn't handle it and remained angry. They could not forgive nor forget all the ugly words spoken by the wife against her husband. This problem would never have occurred had the wife exercised enough self-control to hold her tongue. Had she talked with God, rather than her parents, she and her husband would not now be having this in-law problem.

When Janice and Ralph were first married, she was a pretty girl and weighed about 120 pounds. After ten years of marriage and two children (twins), Janice began putting on weight. It didn't seem to bother her a bit, and when someone remarked to her about it, she would just laugh. Her husband and her children were embarassed about her weight, now 200 pounds. They tried to share their concern with her, but she would just laugh it off. One day while we were discussing her home problems, it dawned on Janice that she was rebelling against Ralph and really did want to have him embarassed by her weight. It was her way of "getting back" at him for not showing her enough love and attention. Instead of confronting him, she just let the problem go on.

21

Some women will go on buying sprees. They can't find happiness in their home, and so they buy things to make them happy. Then when they get tired of the things they bought—they go buy more things.

We had a friend who was a Colonel in the Army, and he and his wife were stationed on the island of Guam. He wrote home to us that though he really loved his wife, he was having a problem with her. She was a compulsive buyer. One day she went out and bought a $1,000 silver service and brought it home. Up to this point, he had not said anything about the many, many needless items she had bought, but this was too much! He wanted to know what was wrong with her.

This is an example of some women who try to find fulfillment in things. Also, it is a way to get revenge against their husbands, to get them into debt way over their heads. Such women have an attitude of "I'll show you for neglecting me." They don't realize that the best way to handle their problems is to confront their husbands and try to solve them directly. Getting him into debt and causing more stress on the marriage and having a vindictive attitude is an inappropriate and unhelpful way to handle them.

Many women go to work outside their home, taking the attitude, "You go your way, and I'll go mine." They get involved in their work and forget about husband, children, and home. Sometimes this even leads to becoming involved with another man.

I talked recently with a young girl who has only been married three years. She began complaining about her husband and how everything was his fault and she didn't love him any more. She told me that the reason she married him was because she was pregnant at the time. We worked through the guilt of her premarital sex by using the Scripture in the fifth chapters of Romans.

> But God showed his great love for us by sending Christ to die for us while we were still sinners. And since by his blood he did all this for us as sinners, how much more will he do for us now that he has declared us not guilty? (Romans 5:8-9 TLB).

As the Holy Spirit began to do His work in her heart, tears came to her eyes and convicted her of the extramarital sex in which she was now involved. She confessed her affair with a man whom she had met at work. She asked Jesus Christ to come into her heart and thanked Him for forgiving her of this and of all her sins. I could tell that even though she had engaged in premarital sex, and even though she was now involved in extramarital sex, she still loved her husband, and this alone was enough to salvage their marriage. Up to this time, because she had not known Jesus Christ and His marvelous grace, she was hoping her husband would beat her up or put her out so she could rationalize her situation and blame him for her wrong actions. To be sure, she could not cope, without Christ's help, with a husband who was out of order. However, she made the problem worse by confiding in someone with whom she worked, giving this other man the love her husband rightfully deserved.

Some women, when they are frustrated, are very vulnerable to the opposite sex. This is why it is so important for women to share their thoughts and feelings with their husbands and their Heavenly Father. They could go to a physician, a minister, a neighbor, a fellow worker, or someone else, but what they are telling others, they should be telling their own husbands. A wife's husband is her counselor, and she reverences him by relating to him as her priest.

> Nevertheless let every one of you in particular so love his wife even as himself; and the wife see that she reverence her husband (Ephesians 5:33 KJV).

A woman reverences her husband by being honest with him and open about herself. She shows respect to him by confiding in him and not in other people.

How embarrassing it must be for a husband to overhear someone relating the details of an intimacy that took place between him and his wife.

When you married your husband, you chose him to be your counselor and your guide. Now respect him by confiding in him. But, you say, he doesn't listen. I know. There are many wives who feel like they are talking to a brick wall. But that isn't any excuse to expose your personal problems to the world. God listens. How many times have you talked with Him lately about your problem? If you go to your husband with an attitude of helplessness he will be only too glad to listen. But if you go to him with the attitude, "He doesn't care anyway," it will come through, and sure enough, he won't care.

Some women won't talk with their husbands and they use "he won't listen" as an excuse. But the truth is, they don't want his help or his counsel or guidance. They want to be independent, and they like the feel of the martyr role. It's fun blaming him for all the trouble.

I have a friend who is a minister's wife. She gave a beautiful testimony of how you can reverence your husband even though he is unresponsive to problems in the relationship. This is her story:

> One of the ladies in the congregation came to me and told me she had "feelings" for my husband. She said she prayed for him all the time. I felt uneasy, but replied, "Well, he sure can use the prayer." I was upset with this woman who came into my home and left this burden with me. I gave her a third person hypothesis, and when I finished, she said, "Oh, you make me feel so dirty." And she left the house in a rush. I indeed intended for her to feel dirty, as she certainly didn't have healthy thoughts on her mind.
>
> I went to my husband some weeks later as the burden got too heavy for me to bear and told him. He just laughed and told me not to worry as he couldn't stand the woman anyway. But being a woman, I couldn't keep quiet, and it bothered me every time I saw this woman, and every time I saw her come out of the church or hang around after every Bible study and church service. I continued to talk with my husband, but he somehow couldn't help me. Fact is, I began feeling like he was beginning to like the woman. She certainly threw herself at him enough. Being an egotistical man, he felt flattered.

By that time, there was no one, absolutely no one, I could confide in but God. So I turned to prayer, praying my husband would see the light and praying for my burden to be lifted. I realized in our twelve years of marriage I had been idolizing my husband instead of seeking God first. I continued to reverence my husband, knowing what he was up to and what he was doing. Thank God I reverenced him, because my prayer was answered and my husband came through. But had I confided in anyone, my husband's ministry would have been ruined. Also I would have been prone to listen to worldly advice and possibly leave him.

But I continued to listen to God and praise Him, and He has worked out this problem in our marriage. My husband is a stronger, more mature man, and his weakness for other women is gone.

Through this experience, I have learned to put the Lord first in my life and claim His promises and all these other things have been added unto me. Thank God I learned to love my husband enough to reverence him and confide only in him and God. Of course, I went through hell itself in dealing with this problem. I suppose I went through every emotion in the book, but God has given me the protection I need and given my husband the strength to be a better witness to His word.

Now this lovely lady didn't have help from her husband, yet she continued to talk with him and with the Lord. Note particularly her comment that had she confided in anyone else, she would have been prone to listen to worldly advice and would possibly have left her husband. Don't you see what sharing with people other than your husband could cause? Of course, then you could blame the other people for giving you the wrong advice. But with God, you cannot fail. He won't let you down.

You see, we have a choice. We can make a right choice by turning to God and asking His guidance, or we can make a wrong choice by seeking attention and understanding in another way.

"Darn it all Mary, if you don't quit talking about your job so much and your boss and all your problems, I think I'll go crazy. I know you have a college education and a degree and make more money than I do, but do you have to keep rubbing it in? You know I don't want you to work. I want you to look after the kids and keep house. I didn't marry a career woman. I married a sweet young thing that promised to be my wife and the mother of my children. I am sick and tired of your job talk and losing yourself in your work. If you gave our home half the time you put in your work, I believe I could cope."

"But Jim, you knew I had a degree when we married. You didn't seem to mind when I went back to work, and especially when I offered to put you through college."

"I know, but I was just trying to please you. Naturally, I felt inferior with you having a degree, but gosh, I make a heap more money now, and you don't have to work. Can't you see what you are doing to our marriage? You are trying to overpower me in the money-making and the decision-making, and you have no interest in our children or home. All I am asking is for you to stop working and let me be the man I am supposed to be. Let me be the breadwinner."

This type of conflict goes on in our American homes more than we wives would like to admit. So many wives go to work to try to get out of the home and end up with the home in turmoil.

> But be sure in deciding these matters that you are living as God intended, marrying or not marrying in accordance with God's direction and help, and accepting whatever situation God has put you into (I Corinthians 7:17 TLB).

Chapter 5

How To Cope

"I just can't take my husband running around with another woman," cried Esther. "How do I cope?"

"Are you a Christian?" I asked.

"No. I've gone to church all my life, but I've never invited Jesus into my heart, because I'm not good enough," she sobbed.

"You asked a very good question about how you can cope with your situation—so let me explain it this way," I replied as I asked for God's guidance in a quick mental prayer. It popped into my mind to say, "Take each letter in the word cope, and it gives us our answer. The letter C stands for Christ, the letter O stands for only, the letter P stands for provides, and the letter E stands for everything. So—Christ Only Provides Everything." As she sat there, desperately looking for some meaning to her life, I continued, "By accepting Him as your Savior and inviting Him into your life, He will guide you and give you the power to cope with your husband's infidelity and anything else that comes along."

"I want to, but I'm afraid God won't accept me the way I am,"

27

she exclaimed.

"You don't need to be afraid," I replied. "He accepts anyone who turns to Him."

"I won't be like Helen Brown, will I?" she asked. (Helen was a tiresome person in the community who would go from one kick to another and was of lately on a religious kick. She talked Christ but did not live Christ.)

"I'm quite sure you will not be like Helen," I assured her, as we prepared to pray.

"Okay, I'm ready then," she said as she smiled, "but you pray first."

The warmth of the Spirit of God was in the living room, and it was especially bright as I prayed, "Lord, Esther and I come into Your presence, thanking You for Your love and mercy. Father forgive me of my sins and cleanse my heart and fill me full of Your love and Holy Spirit. Thank You, Father, for the opportunity of sharing Your love with Esther. I ask You now to cleanse her heart and fill her with Your love and Holy Spirit. Give her also the power to forgive her husband. I pray for Andy wherever he is that You will convict his heart of his wrongdoing and bring him back to Esther. In Jesus name . . ."

Then Esther prayed, "Lord, forgive me of all my sins, and forgive me for hurting all those people all over town. Jesus, I ask You to come into my heart and fill me with Your love and Holy Spirit. I thank You for saving me and helping me to cope. I pray for Andy that he will come back home to me and the children and that he, too, will find You as his Savior . . . I guess that's about it for now, Lord. Thanks! Amen."

Esther's prayers were indeed answered. She did not turn out like Helen; she found the power of the Holy Spirit to help her cope, and her husband did find Christ also as his Savior and Lord. The two of them became a living witness to the wonder and power of God.

When I use the term, "be in Christ," I mean that you are to allow the Holy Spirit to guide your thoughts, your ideas, your thinking. Pray continually. Praise the Lord in all things. Quit griping, as it says in I Corinthians:

> And don't murmur against God and his dealings with you, as some of them did, for that is why God sent his Angel to destroy them (I Corinthians 10:10 TLB).

Use the principle of praise in your life. Give praise to God for your situation, right now, just as it is, whether good or bad.

> Always be joyful. Always keep on praying. No matter what happens, always be thankful, for this is God's will for you who belong to Christ Jesus (I Thessalonians 5:16-18 TLB).

Do you believe in prayer? I remember one time my husband did something that really hurt my heart. I didn't think I would ever be able to forgive him. I prayed all afternoon. I said, "Lord, just let Page see what he has done to me. Lord, just let him see my hurt and make him see it so clearly that he will get sick and want to throw up after he realizes what he has done to me." (This may sound selfish, but I had to pray the way I felt, and that was the truth.) I prayed this all Friday, and Page came and went and nothing changed. That night when we got into bed, he turned to me and asked, "Well, whom do you feel we ought to pray for tonight?" (It is our custom to hold hands and pray for someone or something, in agreement, each night.)

"I want to pray for you," I cried bitterly.

"Me? What's wrong with me?" he questioned with a degree of uneasiness.

We then began to discuss what was going on in my heart. Three hours of talking and arguing finally gave Page an insight into what he had done to hurt me and he exclaimed, "I see it!" He jumped up out of the bed and dashed for the bathroom. "I think I'm going to throw up."

"Hallelujah," I shouted.

He couldn't understand why I was so happy about his throwing up. Then I leveled with him about my prayer. "I prayed you would do that as a sign of your being able to see what you had done to me and the Lord."

If you want your husband changed, set the example by being in Christ and continuing to pray for him, and God will answer your prayers. Remember the prayer of faith can move mountains. I know what you are thinking—"You just don't know how big a mountain my husband is."

> And some women, through faith, received their loved ones back again from death (Hebrews 11:35 TLB).

Your husband may be dead to you and to your family by not taking his responsibility in the home, but I cannot stress enough the power of prayer. If we women spent as much time in prayer as we do in gossiping or complaining, just think of the strength our homes would have today.

When you pray, you never know just how it will be answered. But pray and ask God's guidance for your home, your husband, and yourself. Don't pray as one wife put it, "While I was in my room praying, 'Lord, change Bill,' he was in the den praying, 'Lord, change Carmen.'" Pray God will change you and make you the Christian wife He wants you to be, and then your husband will change, because it is God's promise that we will win them by our godly example.

> Wives, fit in with your husbands' plans; for then if they refuse to listen when you talk to them about the Lord, they will be won by your respectful, pure behavior. Your godly lives will speak to them better than any words (I Peter 3:1-2 TLB).

I know one wife whose husband was out of divine order, and she began praying that God would so change her that it would cause her husband to get in order and love her as Christ loved the church. This young woman did not realize what she was asking for, because God, in answering her prayer, revealed to her that her husband was involved with another woman. Although she was deeply hurt, the young wife began checking up on her husband. She was able to confront him in love with his misbehavior. The couple had many problems to work out, but because she was in Christ, she was able to forgive her husband, and he came under God's divine order. Today they are a testimony for the Lord.

When you pray, you do so because you have a vital relationship with God. Talk with Him as if He were your Father sitting right there beside you. Learn to be honest with God, naming things by their right names. It is easy to say, "Forgive me, Father." But you must say what you feel. "Forgive me, Father for being such a stinker today and acting so childish." "Father, I feel so angry. I am so mad at my husband. Show me how to deal with it."

I was telling a friend on the phone one day how to pray. She, being a new Christian, felt uncomfortable with prayer. I tried to explain, "Just talk with God as you are talking with me, telling me what you feel and what you think." To get my point across, I said, "When I hang up, just keep the phone in your hand and talk out loud to God."

She laughed and said, "Oh you're putting me on."

"No," I said, "try it." We hung up, and a half hour later, my phone rang and it was Linda.

"It worked," she said. She told me how she kept the phone to her ear and kept praying out loud to God, and He revealed to her how to handle her problem. It just came to her what to do. She was so excited. She said her little girl came in ten minutes later and asked if she were still talking on the phone. She answered, "No, I am talking with God."

31

Be sure that you explicity confess your sins so that you can be in fellowship with the Father when He hears you pray.

> If we confess our sins to him, he can be depended on to forgive us and to cleanse us from every wrong (I John 1:9 TLB).

I visited a home not too long ago where the young wife was quite depressed. She sat rocking one small baby, and another toddler was at her knee. Her marriage wasn't going right, her husband wasn't mature, they didn't have any money, and she was miserable. We talked about her relationship with the Lord, and I discovered she was a Christian. I shared with her how to talk with God about her feelings, her frustrations, her hurts, her desires, and her hopes. I told her to talk with God all day long and to pray for her husband that he might come to know God in a personal way. I saw this young woman several weeks later and hardly recognized her. She was radiant. Her pretty blonde hair was gleaming. She kept saying how much God was blessing their home. Her whole attitude had changed toward her marriage and her husband. She was so exciting to talk with I knew she was spending much time talking to God.

Why is it that we have such a hard time going to God with our problems? We are smart enough to go to the doctor for physical ailments or to the lawyer for legal problems. If God created us and has a plan for our lives, why wouldn't we want to confide in Him? One reason is sometimes we don't want to change. Another is we say we don't want to bother God. But that is why He made us, for Him to enjoy us. How can God enjoy us if we don't ever talk with Him? Most of the time our real reason is that we have our minds already made up, and just want Him to bless our decision.

Annie was all confused. She had been married for seventeen years and had four children and she was miserable. Her husband was one of those "good guys." According to Annie, he was "too good for God."

She couldn't stand living with this self-righteous, egotistical, proud, selfish person. She went every route she could think of—getting sick, losing herself in her work, eating too much, spending too much. She would try and talk with her friends about her unhappiness. Their advice was to get out of the marriage if she was so unhappy. Annie made up her mind. She decided to divorce her "too good" husband. She did go for counseling, but she wouldn't listen; her mind was made up.

She started the divorce proceedings, and it was a hot and heavy battle as the husband contested the divorce, claiming he really loved Annie. The final blow for Annie was when her husband won the case. He got the house, the children, and Annie. She was furious. She didn't want the marriage, and she couldn't get out of it. I talked with her.

"Annie, you must realize that you needed to pray about your decision." .

Annie bawled, "I did pray. God wanted me to sue for divorce."

"When did you pray, Annie? After you had already made up your mind?"

I knew Annie was a Christian and knew Bible doctrine. I also knew if she were praying to God that He could have changed her heart about her husband.

Annie finally confessed she had already made up her mind and was just praying for forgiveness, and yet she was determined not to change her mind or her attitude.

Since she had lost the case, I again tried to get her to turn to God and confess that maybe she made a mistake. Maybe God wanted her broken, as she was really at rock bottom. But Annie is too mad and too childish to change and is enjoying her misery. I pray that some day she will grow up, so that God can show her His plan for her life.

The essence of being able to cope with any given situation is a personal and positive relationship with Christ who provides us with a relaxed mental attitude. It is our attitude toward God and

His plan for our lives as it is revealed in Christ and the written Word that gives a person the ability to face every issue with faith and power to change things for the better.

Every wife and mother exercises either a positive or negative influence on her home life. What is it that makes the difference? The difference between a positive or negative force in each circumstance of married life depends upon the woman's choice. If most of her decisions are based upon her desire to please God, then she will have a positive influence upon her husband and children. Her negative influence comes across as she chooses to live unto herself, to put herself first, or her husband first, or her children first. It is in this way that she disobeys the laws of God and becomes an idolater, often without even knowing it.

Many women quite naturally begin their marriage with an attitude of reverence toward their husband; they often literally "worship" him. They make decisions based upon what will please the husband, not God. They think about him all the time, they can hardly stand being away from him. They think the sun rises and sets on him and that there is not anything he cannot do. Such a wife responds to her husband with all that is within her, mentally, emotionally, and physically. And that is as it should be—as long as she has at the center of her life a personal relationship with the living God as her Heavenly Father. If she has not placed God in the center of her life, she soon finds this early reverence turning into idolatry, which over a period of years sours and distorts the marriage.

There is a divine order in marriage, and when this is overlooked all kinds of surprises are in store for us. When we set our husbands up as gods, we set ourselves up for frustration after frustration. The harder we try to come into subjection to our husbands, the harder we cry—simply because we are out of line with God's order.

When we discover that the man we married is made of clay is bent out of shape, we quite naturally usurp the divine role of trying to bend him back—to our own satisfaction.

A woman's fulfillment cannot come in her husband unless she is first fulfilled in Christ. It is in Christ that she receives the gifts of the Holy Spirit and the fruit of the Spirit that enable her to cope. The negative force of a woman's own pride tends to wreck a husband-wife relationship, whereas the positive force of the Holy Spirit tends to build a solid and fruitful husband-wife relationship.

I'm thinking now of a woman who is about to celebrate her twenty-fifth wedding anniversary with an aching heart because her husband is such a frustration to her. Because of her pride, she has protected him over the years, backed him up in his bad decisions, covered for him in his neglect of responsibility, and held things together when he let them fall apart. Now her husband, in his outer role in society, has quite a heavy adult responsibility, yet in his inner person, he responds to situations as a child. So now the wife feels trapped. If she stops supporting her husband, he will fall and she with him. Yet if she continues to worship him in this warped way, without correcting him, he will never mature.

In this case, part of the correctional technique may be not to remind him of his commitments, not nag him into being some-place on time, not cover for his mistakes, not go along with his bad decisions. As a result, people will see him for the first time as he is (a phony) and their loss of respect for him will motivate him to grow up.

What is a woman to do in the light of such a predicament? Should she shrug her shoulders and do nothing? Should she rebel and do all kinds of crazy things like take drugs, become an alcoholic, have an affair, or get emotionally.or mentally sick?

The following chapters will describe the love route, the only way that leads to lasting and laudable wedlock. Before you begin reading them, let me suggest that you make use of the following prayer:

> Lord have mercy on me. I have hated my husband, felt sorry for myself, and strayed far from You. I wanted my husband to

straighten up so that life would be easier for me, not so that You would be glorified. Please forgive me.

Give me grace to release him fully to You. Help me to stop lying to cover his sins. Assist me to stop trying to be his protector. I give You permission to do whatever You must to make him into the man You want him to be.

But, Lord, I'm the one who needs Your help to change most desperately. Give me a heart to cling to You in trusting submission. I thank You for the mess that my marriage is in and I accept my share of the responsibility for it. I thank You for the way that mess has driven me to You as You've opened my eyes to see it. I give You permission to do whatever You must to make me into the woman You want me to be.

I praise You for Your steadfast love that has brought me to this point. And I thank You for the sacrifice of Christ and the gift of the Holy Spirit which have availed for me and will continue to avail for me. *Amen.*

Chapter 6

Who Helps Who?

Be the helpmeet you were created to be, and don't rebel against your role. Sometimes we wives don't want to be used of God.

> And the Lord God said, "It isn't good for man to be alone; I will make a companion for him, a helper suited to his needs" (Genesis 2:18 TLB).

We know well enough that little girls usually mature faster than little boys, and women are often more mature than men. Know this and deal with it.

When your husband acts childish, let him know it.

I was talking with a friend the other day about how childish husbands can be, and she related this story.

She had finished getting dinner ready, and she called her husband and children to the table to eat. She has a twenty-two-month-old daughter, and a four-year-old little boy. The family sat down to eat, and after the husband asked the blessing, the little boy began acting up. The father scolded him, but the little fellow continued to act up. The father got angry and jumped up from the table taking the little fellow with him into another room where the father spanked the child. The wife waited awhile and called for the little boy to come to the table to eat his dinner. He obediently came back and slid into his chair. Meanwhile, the husband was still in the other room sulking over the matter. The wife called to her husband to come on back and eat his dinner, too. He didn't come. Then, realizing how childish he was being and what a poor example he was setting for the children, she said, "Murray, come in here right this minute and eat your dinner." He finally responded, walked into the room, she winked at him, and he got the point. She was forced into the mother role because her husband was acting like a child. Later that evening as they discussed the incident, the husband admitted his childishness and recalled that as a child when he got upset at the table he would always go off and sulk and not eat. His parents never made him come back to the table, so many times he would end up going to bed sulking and hungry. He realized that he was still in his childish behavior pattern. He decided to change so that he could set a good example for his own children. He did not want them to grow up without growing mature.

Reverence your husband. Be his helpmeet. No one loves him more than you do. You are one flesh; if he does not grow in grace, it hinders the Christian witness of the whole family. Always confront him, and be honest about how you feel and what you think. Be sure to tell him the truth about your feelings and then allow him the opportunity to make the decision as to how he will respond to it.

If your husband gives you a gift for some occasion, and you feel that it is inappropriate and that you will not use it—then love him enough to tell him how you feel about it.

One Christmas, many years after we were married, I received as a gift from my husband a gold necklace with a little rounded perfume container attached to it. When I opened it, I did not know whether to laugh or cry—it was horrible. But when I looked at Page's expectant face, I knew he wanted me to oooh and aaah over it—but I just could not. It was not my "style" nor my "scent." What was I to do? Should I accept it and praise him for something I did not intend to wear, or should I tell him the truth about how I felt? Later that day, when we were alone, I said, "Page, I won't hurt your feelings if I tell you something about that necklace you gave me today, will I?"

"Of course not," he replied with an air of self-righteousness.

"Page, I really appreciate the gift, but you do know I don't wear that type of jewelry, and besides, you know I have a favorite perfume that I have worn for years. I can't believe you would buy me something that you knew I wouldn't like."

Page said that he knew I didn't wear that kind of jewelry, and he knew my favorite perfume, but a saleslady came by the house selling cosmetics, and he felt sorry for her and made the purchase. Now my question is: Whom should he feel sorry for? Here I am his wife that he has to live with. Why not please me and show love to me, rather than try to impress some other woman?

Picky, you say? Indeed not. I want you to know my husband has learned how to buy gifts that I will appreciate, and he feels pleased to give. By the way, he had the woman exchange the necklace and got his money back.

I talked with one wife the other day whose husband brought home a small television set for Mother's Day. Now she and I had been talking about confronting, so she decided to confront. She sweetly asked her husband, "Is that television set for you or for me?"

"It's for you," he replied.

"But, I don't want it. We have two in the house now. I think you bought that one for you and your new camper."

He wouldn't readily admit it, but on Monday morning he returned the set, and they both laugh over it now. They are learning to confront, and it saves a lot of resentment later on.

We are even learning to speak the truth in our family. The other day my teenage son Perry brought home a large pack of gum. Knowing I like to chew gum, he said, "Here."

I quickly replied, "Is that gum for you or for me?" He got the point and said it was for him.

Now you may say, "I feel guilty about confronting, especially about a gift." But don't feel that way. When the truth comes out, chances are you'll find your husband gave you something he hadn't put any thought into. If he gives you something that is not you, you can be pretty sure he really didn't have you in mind when he got it. So confront—because you have him in mind when you open it.

Love him enough to confront him. If he always wants to go golfing or fishing with the boys when there are things to do around the house, let him see how selfish he is. Let him know where his priorities are.

Don't let him make you feel guilty. Perhaps he has bought you several things lately, or not scolded you when you bought things for yourself, so now you say, "Well, he deserves to go off with the boys."

Don't you see his game? He is justifying his actions and hoping you'll agree. This is the least you can do for him. But do you need all that stuff? Be honest. Wouldn't you rather have him home mowing the lawn or helping you decorate the den and paint the front steps?

> Stop lying to each other; tell the truth, for we are parts of each other and when we lie to each other we are hurting ourselves (Ephesians 4:25 TLB).

Be his helpmeet. Help him see his responsibility. Don't feel guilty. Calmly confront him with what you feel no matter what it is, but be sure your attitude and your motives are right. Don't let him go and then seethe all afternoon and sulk all evening. It isn't fair to yourself or to your husband.

If you are angry, don't sin by nursing your grudge. Don't let the sun go down with you still angry—get over it quickly; for when you are angry you give a mighty foothold to the devil (Ephesians 4:26-27 TLB).

Know your husband. When we were in seminary, on Tuesday nights the recreation room was open for skating for the family. We would take our children over and let them skate and watch them and admire their progress. One night while we were watching we noticed a fellow, who was somewhat older than we were, with his two children, a little girl about seven and a little boy about five. The little girl was in the middle of the ring (the area for those who do not know how to skate), going back and forth, squatting down on her skates and falling, and picking herself up and falling again. Some of the other parents were helping to pick her up. Meanwhile, the little boy was sitting in the corner with his skates on, crying for help from his father because he could not skate.

As we watched, the father of the two was having a ball, weaving in and out, tagging all the teenage girls (which was not permitted), and pulling down some of the fellows as he raced by. He was the biggest child out there, and it was really pathetic to watch. I wondered what his wife would have felt had she known what he was doing. In all probability she had entrusted the children with him for the evening, and instead of assuming his responsibilities, he was acting like a child and having his own good time, while the children were miserable.

Let's face it—sometimes men can be childish. The other day I had to attend a luncheon. Because I knew I would not be home for lunch I left some homemade potato soup (Page's favorite) in the refrigerator. I had an enjoyable afternoon at the luncheon, but when I arrived home at 5:00 p.m. (which was rather late), Page had already come in. When I sat down, he mumbled, "I don't suppose you're too hungry are you?"

"Not really," I answered.

"I have a headache," he complained after a little while.

"Oh, I'm sorry," I responded.

"When is dinner?" he asked.

"I'm planning dinner for about six o'clock when Perry gets home," I answered.

"I didn't come home for lunch and haven't eaten anything all day," he said with irritation in his voice. "I think I'll go pick us up some spareribs at the Piggly Wiggly," he said.

"That's an idea," I said. He called the grocery and learned they were out of spareribs.

"I'll go get us some hamburgers," he suggested.

"Okay, but I'll have dinner ready in about an hour."

"No," he retorted, "I'll go get us a hamburger."

"Fine," I replied.

He sat down and rocked awhile in silence.

I finally said, "Why don't you just say so, and I'll get your dinner ready now? You have been pouting childishly ever since I walked in the door. Why didn't you just say that you did not eat any lunch and that you would like to eat right away?"

"Because you would have fussed at me for not eating that soup," he answered.

"You're right, Page," I said, "you are a big boy now, and you should have taken time to come home to eat."

"All right, Patti," he agreed, "I should have taken care of myself, and I should have eaten what you fixed, and I have been acting very childishly. Will you forgive me? I was wrong!"

This is an illustration of how I was able to help my husband see his childish behavior. You too can do this and help your husband to become more adult in his attitudes and a great deal more enjoyable to live with.

So be a helpmeet. But to be one you have to be "in Christ," otherwise you will rebel at the thought of helping your husband constantly. Like reminding him to pick up his clothes and throw away his candy wrappers, to clean up his refreshment dishes or glasses after he finishes a snack. Be firm, just as you would be with the children, and hold on to your principles in order to help him to grow up.

Keep after him to pick up his own things. Don't take the easy way out and do it for him or he'll never grow up. The same is true with those habits of his that bug you and make you look bad in the sight of others, because you and your husband are one. Those little habits like picking his nose, or putting cigarette ashes in his cuff, or chewing gum with great gusto, or pulling his glasses off and on. Any little habit that makes him look bad. You want to help him look good. So love him enough to keep after him. If you are in Christ, you can do it in a sweet way that won't come over like nagging, but will sound helpful, and he will get the point. I am afraid most of us wait until we are at our wits' end before we try to talk with our mates, and it comes out like nagging or badgering.

I know one wife whose husband had the habit of flipping his long hair. It really bothered her, but she was afraid to mention it to him. One day her husband came home from the office very upset. His boss had called him in and lectured him about his habit of flipping his long hair and told him that it looked feminine. Now, coming from his boss, that was hard to take. He told his wife about this rebuke and asked her if she had realized he had the habit of flipping his hair. "Yes," she told him and added that it had bothered her to see him do it but she hated to always be on his back about something. He replied that he wished she had told him, it would have been easier to take such a criticism from her than from his boss.

Another thing we women have to realize is that men have a hard time expressing their feelings, and we must patiently help pull them out. The male child is taught from infancy not to cry or show emotions or reveal his inner thoughts. Therefore, when he becomes an adult, he does not know how to express these inner thoughts. And sometimes he does not want to express these inner thoughts because he feels they make him look weak, or perhaps his inner thoughts are not healthy, or are even evil.

One wife was always criticizing everything and everyone, and her husband would just sit there and nod and say nothing. Some months later, when they were having marital problems and came for counseling, he admitted he liked hearing his wife criticize others, and usually agreed with her, but he thought she looked bad for expressing those thoughts. So he just let her express them for him, too, and he kept his good public image. This was especially the case if they were in a group. His wife would sound off on something, and she would almost hang herself with extreme statements and even though he agreed with her, he would not back her up, because he didn't want to look bad.

We wives need to open our hearts to our husbands whenever they offer to share their feelings. You may think your husband is wrong sometimes—that he shouldn't feel the way he does or shouldn't have gotten so angry when his boss criticized his work or when his mother gave the family antique to his little sister—but hear him out anyway. If we want our husbands to communicate with us, we need to show compassion and love. We should try to be sympathetic even when we don't agree with him.

For example, suppose your husband has a disagreement with his mother. He says, angrily, "I can't ever seem to do anything right."

Even though you silently side with your mother-in-law, you should support your husband by saying, "I'm glad to know how you feel, but what do you think is the problem?"

Once he has expressed his inner thoughts on the subject, you might say, "I don't completely agree with you, but I am pleased you wanted to discuss it with me."

This is what psychologists call "positive reinforcement." By showing appreciation when he does open up, you encourage him to open up more.

We can also help the communication between our children and their father. "See how daddy feels about it; he really knows about that subject." It will help your husband to relate to his child.

Encourage your husband to express his feelings. The need for this is hard for us women to realize at times, because we usually say what we think and feel. Men are not as expressive. We need to pray for patience until we can get our husbands to open up. Don't be shocked or suprised when he makes a statement. Very calmly ask him what he is feeling about it. Help him to open up.

A marriage is built on relationships, and if there is no communication between the two with regard to feelings, thoughts, and ideas, there can be no relationship. You cannot change your husband, but you can make it easier for him to open up and discuss his fears, joys, and disappointments. If you can both share your strengths and weaknesses, it will make him a better man and you a better woman.

I know what you are thinking. "When I took him for 'better or worse' I didn't know how 'worse.' I didn't know I would have to train him along with my children." That is a rebellious attitude. Just confess it, repent, and move on.

I suppose if we wives could see our role from God's viewpoint, it would help us have a better attitude. You see, when we married we made a covenant:

> I take thee to be my wedded husband, to have and to hold from this day forward, for better, for worse, for richer, for poorer, in sickness and in health, to love and to cherish till death us do part, according to God's holy ordinance; and thereto I plight thee my troth (faithfulness).

Now we didn't know everything we would be getting into. Didn't know how childish our husband could be. Didn't know he had this sexual perversion, didn't know he was a mamma's boy, didn't know he was so insecure, didn't know he really did not have a personal relationship with the Lord Jesus Christ, though he said he did. We didn't know all these things. We didn't know that after some fifteen years of marriage, because of all this, he would have an affair with another woman.

Now, we did not know all of this, it is true, but we did make a covenant—an agreement with our husband and with our Lord, "Till death us do part." Yes, I know what you are thinking, "My husband is 'dead' as far as I am concerned; there is no rapport, no feeling, no response." I am sure that in many marriages one partner is 'dead' to the other. But that can change quickly, especially if you are the one who has cut off communication out of disgust at your spouse's shortcomings.

Honesty and openness is not just the "best" policy—it is the "only" policy within the marriage relationship. There should never be any fact, faith, or feeling that is not expressed to the marriage partner in some terms. When you are married in God's sight you are one; therefore there is no little private world that is to be denied the spouse. Otherwise, you are out of line and out of order, a situation which leads to all kinds of incompatibilities— mental, emotional, sexual, social.

It is sad to see in so many couples whom we counsel the shock of the wife or husband when they hear their mate say something and they respond, "I didn't know you felt that way."

Sometimes our husbands think we can read their minds and know what they are thinking, but the truth is we never really know unless they are willing to be honest about how they feel.

I heard one wife say about her husband who would never talk to her when he was at home, "I can't wait for the phone to ring at night. When my husband has to answer it, I get to hear him talk." Most wives have to learn how their husbands feel about a subject or situation by hearing them express it to someone else, maybe a cute blonde at some party, for example. This is anything but love, and yet husbands wonder why we can't respond sexually. That is the reason. There is no expression of love on the part of the husband when he is not honest with what he feels and thinks about things.

Some may say that the reason husbands do not express themselves is because the wife is too critical, judgmental, opinionated, bossy, or nosy, but this line of argument does not always hold up. If the wife just sat quietly and listened to her "knight in shining armor" tell all (assuming he ever did), without honestly and forthrightly responding to his expression, then she would not only be dishonest, but also forfeit her God-given role as helpmeet and responder. In the beginning, everything that God created was "good" except one thing—man's aloneness:

> And the Lord God said, "It *isn't good* for man to be alone, I will make a companion for him, a helper suited to his needs" (Genesis 2:18 TLB).

God created two "roles" for men and women, interdependent upon each other, neither superior nor inferior, simply different. The battle of the sexes could be easily avoided if each one would open up, be honest, and accept their God-given role in all its splendor and glory.

I heard a man say to a group my husband and I were leading, "But there are some things a man just can't tell his wife." This is like throwing cold water, quenching the fire of love between a man and his wife. What does he have that is so secret that he cannot confide in his wife? This kind of withholding takes away a woman's dignity and personhood and saps the zeal of love from the relationship.

We women are just as guilty if we hold on to our "fantasy worlds" and don't share our thoughts and feelings (good and bad) in the total honesty of commitment. It is true, we are often tempted to go our way and let them go their way, but this is an immature and childish response to the situation. *Someone* has to be mature, and it might as well be you, that is, if you desire a truly happy marriage, one that God will honor and in which He will delight.

Some women grow up feeling unloved because of their childhood or background. Therefore, when they marry, they assume they have no rights and no privileges. They suppress their anger and resentment at past and present circumstances because they don't want to seem ungrateful that their husband chose them to marry. If such women don't drop this dishonest veneer of gratitude and ventilate their feelings, men will exploit their "good will" until there is some explosion.

Other women live in fantasy worlds. These are women who cannot face reality and fantasize about other men who are more attractive and thoughtful than their husbands. They don't really want to deal with their marriage problems, as these problems are an excuse for them to escape into their other world. Some women would rather live in this fantasy of theirs than in reality, and lie, cheat, and steal rather than face the truth about themselves and get help. Usually these women end up having an affair and blame their husbands for driving them to it. But the truth is a woman with persistent problems with fantasy should confide in her husband these wrong thoughts and seek help through prayer.

As a man thinketh in his heart, so is he. (Proverbs 23:7 KJV)

How would you feel if you knew your husband was always dreaming about other women?

Women who get caught up in these fantasy worlds are unstable, can't face themselves, are always rationalizing, will lie, and are basically dishonest not only with others but with themselves. They are women who do not love themselves because they can't face up to what they really are, and can't be honest with their mate about their thoughts and feelings.

Take the case of Barbara. She was a young woman who was full of pride and self-righteousness. She had been divorced and remarried and had never worked through the first marriage. Because of a sexual perversion in her childhood, she was not only unstable but began to fantasize. She would think about herself with other men, about the attention they would give her, and about how they would make love to her. Because her mind was always in this other world, she could not relate well to her present husband. But this also led to her being a big flirt. Women disliked her because whatever group Barbara was in, she was always hanging around the men being flitty and obnoxious. She could always manage to get another man to light her cigarette and brush against his cheek and hold his hand.

The wives of these men would be furious and fuss at their husbands. One woman did find the love to confront Barbara when she found her seated in her husband's lap; she asked Barbara to remove herself and not to ever act that way again in their presence. But because of Barbara's fantasy world, she grew worse and worse.

She went to a church retreat. There she would hold her head high and quote Scripture and play her "church role." But it happened. She began to fantasize she was being loved by the director, and in this fantasy she reached the point where she could not come and go out of her little world at will. Her fantasy began to become fact.

Barbara found excuses to see the director after the sessions. She finally made sexual advances toward him in the chapel one night, and both Barbara and the director ended up in his room. They carried on their affair all through the rest of the retreat.

Now here was a young woman who not only fantasized immorality, but acted it out, thus commiting adultery, stealing another woman's husband, cheating on her own husband, ruining her family, and wrecking the lives of others. Such an abomination to God! All because of a few little thoughts. She is now divorced again and in a mental institution.

This same fantasy world involvement can be a problem for men. There are some men who constantly dream about other women. Men who tease about looking at other women really aren't teasing. They say, "Well at least I am being honest." True, but they don't want to change. You can see why this kind of person would not make a very good marriage partner if he were thinking of someone else other than his wife. If a man looks at another woman lustfully he is committing adultery in his heart (Matthew 5:28).

It's hard for a wife to admit that her husband would be capable of this kind of thinking. But if he is preoccupied a lot, it is not always his work he is thinking about. If your husband never listens to what you are saying, find out what he is thinking about.

I've heard some couples say, "We've been married thirty years and have never quarreled." The fact that they never quarrel does not mean their marriage is healthy and happy. In marriage, a heated verbal exchange of words frequently brings truth to light. Ventilate and expose those deepest feelings—also those hidden hopes and fears.

Some couples don't want to "rock the boat." They don't want to quarrel but just walk away instead. This is childish. You must both face reality and facts, not avoid them.

Sometimes we apply the "silent" treatment. "I just don't want to talk about it." This is just as immature. There is no problem so great that talking it out and praying it through won't work it out.

Love is built on a relationship. If there is no communication in a marriage there is no real love. I have seen some marriages end in divorce. Then the husband really told his wife off, and in the process of opening up, getting off his chest what he had held back for many years, the spark of love was rekindled and, lo and behold, they remarried.

But, back to our role as a helpmeet. If you are a Christian and can see your situation from God's viewpoint, then just relax. God loves you, and He won't let anything happen if you remain in Him and abide in Him. Give your partner all the help he needs, help him mature, and you will reap the rewards. I realize that when you married, you wanted someone to provide for you and protect you and cherish you. That is as it should be. But both of you have a lot of growing up to do. So begin by accepting your helpmeet role and strive to help your husband in all areas. Now I know this can be a drain on you and at times wear thin, but all things are possible through Christ—so claim His promise:

> For I can do everything God asks me to with the help of Christ who gives me the strength and power (Philippians 4:13 TLB).

I know a case right now, a couple I'm counseling, where the husband left a lovely Christian wife for another woman. The wife has remained steadfast, and the husband has finally come home. His wife has forgiven him. Now her responsibility is to maintain a Christian attitude and love for her Lord. This marriage can and will work and even be strengthened. The reason the husband got out of line was because they were unequally yoked. After eight years of marriage, his darkness could not live with her light. When a man is not a Christian, he loves evil and hates good.

> Drink from your own well, my son—be faithful and true to your wife. Why should you beget children with women of the street? Why share your children with those outside your home? Let your manhood be a blessing; rejoice in the wife of your youth. Let her charms and tender embrace satisfy you. Let her love alone fill you with delight. Why delight yourself with prostitutes, embracing what isn't yours? *For God is closely watching you,* and he weighs carefully everything you do (Proverbs 5:15-21 TLB).

When a man comes back to his wife, it is usually only to a loving, praying wife. If she loves him, she will pray for him continually until he sees the light. It is only through her prayer and faith that she will win him.

Chapter 7

The Bedroom and the Upper Room

In the seventh chapter of I Corinthians, Paul plainly states that it is better to marry than to remain single and aflame with desire.

For many years, marriages have had real problems in the area of the sexual relationship. The reason is most people are not yet looking at the sexual relationship from God's point of view. In this day and age, men learn their sexual behavior patterns from *Playboy* philosophy rather than from God's divine viewpoint. Men make women feel very guilty and claim that the sexual problem is the woman's fault—she is frigid. From God's standpoint, there are no frigid women.

> Then God said to the woman, "You shall bear children in intense pain and suffering, yet even so, you shall welcome your husband's affections, and he shall be your master" (Genesis 3:16 TLB).

Therefore, woman is a responder. God made her that way. She responds to attention, praise, kindness, talking to her husband about his ideas, his thoughts, his dreams, his hopes, his desires, his strengths, his weaknesses (if he will admit them—and he needs to if he is planning on having a successful marriage and sexual relationship).

Let's begin with love. God is love. Therefore, if you do not know God personally in the person of the Lord Jesus Christ, you cannot fully experience love. You can lust, but you cannot love. If the husband is not a Christian, and the wife is, then after several years of marriage the sexual relationship will likely degenerate and possibly cease because the man will be entering into the activity in lust. The wife will feel that something is wrong (perhaps not consciously), and thus not be able to respond. Tension begins to mount, and the situation becomes explosive and often ends in the divorce court, neither partner realizing what is happening.

Are you having trouble with your sexual response to your husband? If so, then begin to look for his selfish behavior and get him to check out his relationship to the Lord Jesus Christ. Is it real? Is he changing? Is he growing in grace? A woman responds to love and, if her husband does not show her attention, appreciation, kindness, and affection, she cannot respond sexually.

Don't let your husband make you feel guilty by accusing you of frigidity. God made sex, and the only way for sex to be satisfying is that two people love God and love each other. If a man is not a Christian, he is never fully satisfied sexually, because of his lust pattern. But, if he is a Christian, Christ satisfies him and the sex act is secondary. The same is true for a woman. Thus, the non-Christian is never satisfied sexually. You can see how this would be if the husband were not a Christian and the wife is. The husband would always be wanting sex (lust) and the wife couldn't meet those demands.

If we are to enjoy sex, then we have to see it from God's point of view. When two people come together in marriage they are promising their faithfulness to each other and to God, if both are Christians. Now the sex act is an outward response of an inward

54

joining of the souls of two people together with God.

Love in the true sense of the word is not at all selfish. You put yourself in the husband's place. You seek to understand him and why he is the way he is. There is that special rapport—you "feel" with him.

But men often do not have this special rapport and empathy with their wives but relate only to the wife's body. We women need to be aware of what they are thinking so we can handle such a situation. It is not at all flattering for a wife to think that her husband loves only her body—in fact it could give her a sinking feeling for several reasons:

1. Her body could be, and more than likely is no different than any woman's body. Thus, he could love every other woman's body. This premise could hurt the wife and make her feel insecure, and ultimately, unresponsive.

2. Also a wife knows, somewhere in the back of her mind, that if her husband loves her for her body that her body will not hold up forever. So when they get older, he will probably be looking at all the younger bodies. This is not a very exciting prospect for a wife to ponder.

3. Such body consciousness on the part of the husband puts tremendous pressure on the wife to keep up, to perform, to deliver. If a wife cannot respond to her husband's sexual advances, it places her in a very precarious position—she feels trapped and doomed, and very defeated. She often rebels (she may not know why) in very strange and odd ways, making matters even worse.

4. How devastating to a wife's personhood it would be if she had breast cancer and had to have a breast removed,

knowing that her body was what held her husband's desire. Or if she had some disease that kept her from being able to function sexually—how cruel it would be for a husband to have majored on the "body" and not the "being" of his wife. Certainly he could change his tune—but she would be afraid of not being able to meet his demands and of losing him to some better-equipped female.

I am suggesting that we put the emphasis upon the spiritual union of a man and woman. This gives a whole new concept for sexual behavior. You see when man is born into the kingdom of self, he has natural sexual drives which he must learn to control and direct. But when a man gets married, he gets the mistaken idea that he has now purchased himself a sexual object and all he has to do is control and direct his sexual desire toward this object. His sexual drive is then focused upon this object which he possesses.

Of course, that is an improvement over sexual promiscuity, but it puts the husband-wife relationship on a fleshly level, a carnal level which will not hold up over the years. This kind of relationship is not lasting and eventually breaks down.

Young couples can and do thrive under this carnal relationship in sex for a few years, but sooner or later it becomes quite an issue. A husband's attitude toward his wife as an object for his sexual lust is not a legal crime, but it is a spiritual offense in the eyes of God. A wife who responds to her husband's sexual lust or is taught to do so will be caught in an inner conflict later which she will not know how to resolve. If a couple's marriage is sexually dysfunctional and the wife is mistakenly taught to be more carnally minded, it may work for a while, but eventually they will be back in the same rut. A physical relationship just won't last.

It is only in the spiritual arena of marriage that a lasting and satisfying relationship can be established in the area of sex. A lasting, wholesome, and functional marriage cannot be permanently built around the physical and sexual attraction of male and female. However, exciting, long-lasting sexual fulfillment is the by-product of a husband and wife learning to relate in the realm of the spiritual.

This is why courtship is so exciting for couples who are spiritually minded. If, during the courtship period, the suitor seeks not carnal knowledge but spiritual knowledge from his bride-to-be, she will respond to this attention with trustful desire and will look forward with delight to the time that she can lawfully respond to him sexually. Then as the husband continues to open himself on every level to his wife over the years, she will continue to happily respond sexually as well as emotionally to him. If, on the other hand, the husband's attitude changes, and he begins to place the emphasis upon the physical contact and upon her body, they will soon find the ship of matrimony lodged on a sandbar, run aground. The husband does not know or has forgotten that his wife is sexually aroused and responds to him gladly when she knows *he loves her for her being and not just for her body.*

There may be some wife who would take issue with this concept, but I believe her objection would indicate she has deceived herself into thinking she is sexually stimulated by her husband's lustful advances. If so, she has prostituted her marriage. One woman could never fulfill a man's lust, and if she tries, she will only make him more and more lustful. He will never get enough sex and will have to be satisfied with whoever is available wherever he is.

Marriage is a divine institution because it was instituted by God. It is a holy wedlock because it is based upon the spiritual. It becomes an unholy bedlock when it is based solely upon the physical. The physical wears out and can never hold up for a permanent relationship. So even if a man lusts after his own wife, he is out of line with the divine intention: "Let not sin therefore reign in your mortal body, that ye should obey it in the lusts thereof" (Romans 6:12). Although you are bound into oneness, you are nevertheless free. You are free to question, to seek, to probe, to grow, to give, to listen.

If there is any unconfessed guilt within your husband's heart, you simply will not be able to experience this great quality of love between you. The same goes for you. If you have bitterness, resentment, and disrespect that is not confessed toward your husband, you will not experience true love between you. Love is a blending of two people in marriage into oneness and involves the soul, the body, and the spirit. If either of the marriage partners are unwilling to give out their innermost thoughts, feelings, desires and dreams, strengths and weaknesses, then there cannot be this complete union. This is where the truth comes in—the partners must be open on every level, for the physical union to be holy and pure and undefiled.

> Honor your marriage and its vows, and be pure; for God will surely punish all those who are immoral or commit adultery (Hebrews 13:4 TLB).

You may think that it is the sex act that makes you one. Yes, that is true to a degree, for Paul teaches that from God's viewpoint a man who goes into a prostitute becomes one with her.

> And don't you know that if a man joins himself to a prostitute she becomes a part of him and he becomes a part of her? For God tells us in the Scripture that in his sight the two become one person (I Corinthians 6:16 TLB).

But, for the union of husband and wife to be right, it must be the outward response of an inward reverence, a joining of the soul and spirit of husband and wife together with God.

Men tend to get hung up on the physiological functioning of the sexual activity and stress the technique. Sex, from the divine viewpoint, is an expression of love, which flows naturally from a tender and trusting relationship.

As a wife, you need to confront your husband with this fact and let him know that you cannot respond physically to his sexual advances apart from a tender expression of his love and protection and kindness. There is a great need for honesty at this point, otherwise the sex act for the wife is nothing more than a duty performed which has little or no satisfaction or relevance for the Christian marriage. The sexual activity for both wife and husband is mutually satisfying when based upon divine principles.

Chapter 8

Adultery and Reconciliation

Because of the sexual perversion in the world today, many couples have been misled. As we have pointed out before, God made the sexuality of male and female to be expressed only within the bounds of holy wedlock.

> Don't you realize that your bodies are actually parts and members of Christ? So should I take part of Christ and join him to a prostitute? Never! And don't you know that if a man joins himself to a prostitute she becomes a part of him and he becomes a part of her? For God tells us in the Scripture that in his sight the two become one person. But if you give yourself to the Lord, you and Christ are joined together as one person.
>
> That is why I say to run from sex sin. No other sin affects the body [personal and church] as this one does. When you sin this sin it is against your own body. Haven't you yet learned that your body is the home of the Holy Spirit God gave you, and that he lives within you? Your own body does not belong to you. For God has bought you with a great price. So use every part of your body to give glory back to God, because he owns it (I Corinthians 6:15-20 TLB).

If you or your husband has gone outside the bounds of marriage in an affair with someone else, then reread the above Scripture and confess your sin against God and your spouse and repent. There is no greater sin in a marriage relationship than the sin of adultery. But God will forgive and cleanse the guilt away if you repent, and He will reunite you with your spouse in spirit, soul, and then body. Let's face it, God will not allow us to continue in adultery. Be honest with your spouse and admit your sin.

This is why it is so important for couples to be Christians when they marry. Not that Christians don't ever fall into adultery or "look" upon another woman or man, but they will not be allowed to remain peacefully in that sin because the Holy Spirit will convict their hearts of wrongdoing.

In dealing with adultery, first of all, confess everything to God and to your husband. Be completely honest with him, or you will not be able to live with the guilt and shame. You have nothing to lose and everything to gain.

I talked with one woman who had had an affair, and she said her husband would kill her if he knew. She finally was persuaded to tell him. Oh, yes, it hurt him. But he didn't kill her, and he didn't divorce her. In fact, they are now happily married and a living testimony of the healing power of acting in truth and love.

As you talk with your husband, and he becomes your counselor, he will ask you questions and pull out of you your inner thoughts concerning your actions. Don't take the attitude "what he doesn't know won't hurt him." It will hurt him and hurt you, too. You can never build a relationship on dishonesty.

As your husband talks with you, try to sympathize with what he is going through, his pride, his hurt, his shock. Put yourself in his place. Then realize the situation you were in with the other man. Realize that no matter how many times he told you he loved you or how many times he told you he would divorce his wife, he was just saying that in order to get you to continue in the relationship. He told you he loved you in order to cover up his own guilt. He really was abusing and using you. He only wanted your body and not your being. He had no intention of giving up his wife and children and lovely home and enduring the scandal of divorce.

Statistics show that men who do have affairs usually pick out a woman they consider "lower" than themselves. Perhaps they feel their wife is good and pure. They feel a need to get someone to go for their little game who doesn't have much moral strength or has a weakness in the area of lust. Just know that lust is his main thought.

If you can see this, it will make you hate the evil you have done and therefore not want to enter into another affair again. By seeing that the guy used you, you will more easily be able to forget him and those "feelings" and be free to love your husband who stood by you.

You're probably thinking, "My case is different." But we have counseled with hundreds of couples, and we always get basically the same answer. The process goes something like this: the unhappy housewife seeks counsel from a man other than her husband, develops feelings for him, and before you know it, they are in bed together. To be truthful, most women like this are aggresive and really lead the situation. The man just relaxes and lets her play all the shots.

Men we have counseled with admit that they have had affairs with women whom they did not intend to marry, wouldn't even want to live with and who even repulsed them. And yet the man was selfish enough to overlook these things in pursuit of his own lustful satisfaction. If women could only see this, they would never let themselves get mixed up in this sort of thing. Once you become involved, you become blinded and it is difficult to face the truth.

There is no excuse for adultery, no matter what sort of husband you have. You do not have to make the wrong choice by committing adultery. This is a sin against your own body. God does not forgive excuses. He forgives sin.

Once you have worked through all of this, then you have to work through the associations. We had one fellow tell us after his wife had had an affair, "I wanted to throw up at night when I went to bed. Knowing my wife and her lover slept in it while I was away made me sick."

These associations are hard to work through. Every time you hear a voice or a song or anything that reminds you of the affair, it hurts.

If your husband has committed the sin of adultery against his own body, and you are Christians and trying to work through the experience, then let me give you a few pointers I have picked up from couples who are trying to rebuild their marriages. The aftermath of an affair is like a fire or tornado; there is much damage, and the healing takes a considerable amount of time. Since I am writing to the women, I will use their feelings, although these also express the feelings a man goes through if his wife has been unfaithful.

The following quotations are from women who have gone through the shock and horror of discovering their husbands' unfaithfulness to them. It is a long list, and it covers the gamut of human emotions.

"When I saw my husband giving attention to the other women, I first had feelings of intense love and protection for him. I felt that I was competing for his attention."

"I didn't exactly know what was going on, but I felt terribly insecure, so I wanted to fight for what was mine."

"As I felt my husband's interest and attention slipping from me, I of course felt rejection and the tremendous need to defend myself, which he interpreted as nosy and bossy and 'being out in front.'"

"When I learned that my husband had been unfaithful to me, I felt shock which turned quickly into anger. I told him off and let off the steam."

"I had feelings of hate when my husband told me about his

adultery. I wanted to kill him, hurt him, to fight him."

"My feelings were of despair. . . . I wanted to leave him—just get out of the whole mess."

"I was terribly ashamed that my own husband would do such a thing, that he would allow some other woman to touch him or make love to him. . . . It was sickening."

Knowing the truth about your husband's infidelity is a necessity, but the need of getting out your feelings is also necessary. They are not very easy to confess, but they do need to be expressed in order for healing to take effect. The following are comments we heard from women who needed to say what was in their hearts:

"He thought so little of himself and me to sell his body to that whore."

"He loved me so little as to let himself use another woman's body for his selfish pleasures."

"He lied to me when I questioned him about where he was, so I don't think I can trust him when he talks with other women for fear of his getting involved again."

"I am so jealous of his giving more attention to other women than to me."

"I am worried that he will go back to her if she calls."

"I am so afraid this will be spread all around, yet I want to get even and tell everybody what a sorry, no-account husband he has been, how terrible he's been to me."

"I want him to tell his mother that he isn't the sweet little boy she thinks he is."

"When he is quiet, I am afraid he is thinking of her and how much pleasure he gave her and attention he got."

"When he is away, I am suspicious of where he is—I'm afraid they are meeting again someplace."

"I'm always wondering if he is calling her or if she is calling him to continue the relationship."

"I could not show sweet feelings for him as long as he was unable or unwilling to change in his outlook on his relationship with the other woman, and with all women."

"Every time I see him look at another woman, I wonder what he is thinking or if this may be the next flirtation."

"I get angry and feel very uneasy when I see him enjoying being with other women and flirting with them."

"I am very suspicious of his going out of town or being away any length of time."

"I keep watching his every move to see if I can see any signs of regression or self-pity or depression or rebellion or anything that might lead him away from me."

"I don't enjoy going places with him, to parties or even to church or any social events, for fear he will go back to his old pattern of looking and flirting."

"I want my husband to be attentive to me and aware of my needs and feelings, but he seems to always want to impress the other women."

"I want him to hate what he has done and understand how I feel about his affair so that he will understand how he has abused and misused our marriage and our vows. I want him to renew his promise to me to be faithful, since he has broken his first vows. I want him to repent and change to the point that I can see it and see him following Christ."

These are just a few of the feelings that women have talked with me about after their husbands had had an affair. In talking with the men, we find they have the same feelings, only more intense. Men seem to recover from such an ordeal more slowly than women.

After a couple has worked through the facts and the feelings, they need to examine the associations. The wife must realize that she has to get rid of anything that the other man gave her. She cannot hold onto the past. For her husband's sake and hers, she needs to be honest and do away with anything that reminds her of her past involvement. I know this is asking a lot, for I talked with one couple who had worked through most of the problems together, but when it came to the associations, the wife didn't want to give up a ring and a pin and several other items that her lover had given to her. This nearly killed the husband to realize that, after all he had been through, his wife didn't have the sensitivity to want to get rid of these. As we counseled her, she began to see how wrong being sentimental was. She had to burn her bridges behind her.

This same couple had bought a new jeep station wagon only about six months before, and the husband actually had to get rid of the car because he knew his wife had met her lover and they had had sexual relations there. The husband could no longer drive it or ride in it because of the association it had.

> Let there be tears for the wrong things you have done. Let there be sorrow and sincere grief. Let there be sadness instead of laughter, and gloom instead of joy. Then when you feel your worthlessness before the Lord, he will lift you up, encourage and help you (James 4:9-10 TLB).

Handling the associations in the aftermath of an affair is done only by the grace of God. One man who had had an affair said looking at motel signs tore him up. He had to learn to confess to God it was not the motels that were bad but his own guilt and memories that made them seem that way. When the signs brought up memories, he learned to confess this to God and ask Him to remove the thoughts.

Couples also have to work out some associations together. The person who has been hurt in the partnership needs the comfort and assurance from the one who did the hurting.

Jack and Hilda were good friends with Alice and Ted. The couples got together often, and on Jack and Hilda's fifteenth wedding anniversary, Alice and Ted gave them a silver serving tray. Hilda was so excited. She loved silver and had wished for a serving tray for a long time. Months later, Hilda found out that Jack and Alice were having an affair. After the worst quarrels, arguments, and fights, Hilda and Jack were able to overcome the situation and decided to make a go of their marriage. Yet Hilda had such mixed emotions every time she looked at the silver serving tray—it reminded her of the terrible pain of the affair. Jack wanted to be understanding and suggested they get rid of it and he would eventually try to replace it. It was a hard decision for Hilda for she tried to realize there was nothing wrong with the tray itself. Nevertheless she got rid of the tray and felt much better. She also appreciated Jack's promise to get her another one.

Couples have to deal with the hurt in the same way. A wife whose husband has been unfaithful feels shame. She can't believe her husband would do such a thing, and her pride is hurt. How could he possibly choose someone other than her? She has to confess her hurt and pain to God and ask Him to remove it. She may have to do this a hundred times a day, but it is only by the grace of God that this pain and hurt can be removed. Every time a wife has a thought about her husband lying in bed with that "other woman," she has to confess this painful thought to God and ask him to remove it. God does heal, and God does give grace and mercy to those who seek Him first and ask for His divine guidance.

Forgiveness is not an emotion. It is an attitude. It is a decision. I may say, "I want to forgive you," when I don't feel forgiveness. This is because forgiving is a decision, an act of the will, and not an emotion. Most people want to wait till they feel forgiving before they can forgive. This is an error. You make the decision to forgive first, and then God gives you an inner peace and you can begin to feel better toward the person who has hurt you.

The greatest concern for a godly woman hurt by her husband's adultery is being able to forgive him, because she knows in her heart if she doesn't forgive him, God won't forgive her. It is for God's sake first of all that she forgives and not her husband's.

Your heavenly Father will forgive you if you will forgive those who sin against you; but if you refuse to forgive them, he will not forgive you (Matthew 6:15 TLB).

In the second place, forgiving those who sinned against you stirs within them a desire to repent. But don't try to get them to repent and then forgive them; real forgiveness doesn't look for repentance. The wife who reverences her husband will make the decision to forgive and carry it out whether she feels it or not, and God will honor her efforts.

If you are one of the fortunate couples who has not gone through the experience of infidelity on the part of one or both partners, then praise the Lord and continue to remain faithful and work through all your problems together with God's help. One couple related to us that they had a wonderful marriage and sexual relationship now and for many years. I asked what the reason for their success was and she responded, "Every night before we go to bed we share together the day's activities; we laugh a little, sometimes we cry a little, but we are honest with each other. Then we pray together."

If couples would develop this kind of attitude and habit, how great their marriages would be.

Chapter 9

Inner Light and Outer Beauty

I am sure most books you have read for women on how to love their husbands or be good wives have a chapter on making oneself attractive. To be sure, this helps. But from God's viewpoint it is more critical to a happy marriage to fix up the inside than be attractive outwardly. God looks on the heart. If we love God and mature in Him through prayer and Bible study, we will almost automatically become beautiful on the outside.

> No one lights a lamp and hides it! Instead, he puts it on a lampstand to give light to all who enter the room. Your eyes light up your inward being. A pure eye lets sunshine into your soul. A lustful eye shuts out the light and plunges you into darkness. . . . If you are filled with light within, with no dark corners, then the outside will be radiant too, as though a floodlight is beamed upon you (Luke 11:33-36 TLB).

A woman in Christ will grow more and more radiant. Her eyes will gleam, and her husband will want to follow the gleam. She will be pleasing in her appearance. She will be clean and neat. She will cut out all habits harmful to her health to keep her body pure for the Holy Spirit to dwell in. She will be modest in her apparel, not dressing to get the attention of other men or women, aiming only to please her husband and to be an asset to him.

> Wives, fit in with your husbands' plans; for then if they refuse to listen when you talk to them about the Lord, they will be won by your respectful, pure behavior. Your godly lives will speak to them better than any words. Don't be concerned about the outward beauty that depends on jewelry, or beautiful clothes, or hair arrangement. Be beautiful inside, in your hearts, with the lasting charm of a gentle spirit which is so precious to God. That kind of deep beauty was seen in the saintly women of old, who trusted God and fitted in with their husbands' plans (I Peter 3:1-5 TLB).

Because of this radiant personality and because of her love for the Lord, she will be beautiful inwardly and outwardly. She will have the inner enthusiasm to fix herself up and be neat and clean and attractive. This goes for children and family also. Have you ever seen a woman all dressed up "fit to kill," all "vogue on the outside and vague on the inside," yet her little children running along behind her have shoes on the wrong feet, runny noses, tangled hair, and dirty faces? A truly good wife would not permit this to happen in her home. She would see that her whole family is clean, and neat.

Being godly also provides the wife with the power to keep a clean and orderly home. Because God is a God of order, when you come to know Him and His ways, you come into order. You begin to think ahead. You keep track of your social and business schedules as well as your husband's, so that he won't get up one morning unable to find the blue shirt that goes to the blue suit because it is in the clothes hamper. He will be proud to bring home business associates, because he knows you keep a clean house. He will be able to run home the last minute for lunch and come home to a clean house, one that doesn't smell of dirty diapers and fish cooked the night before because the dirty dishes are still in the sink. He will be likely to spend more time at home when the house is clean and in order. No man, or anyone else for that matter, likes to walk into a house that has a bad odor and looks like a hurricane just hit it.

Maybe you're thinking you can't keep it clean because of the kids and all. But this is where the organized mother comes in; by that I mean you keep everyone organized. See to it that the children pick up after themselves. If they leave dishes or clothes and books all over the place, make them pick them up immediately. Mothers, teach your girls to help you. Be an example to them in everything you do. How else do you think they will learn to become organized wives when they marry?

Another characteristic of the Christian wife is that she is on time. She sees to it that she is ready for the meeting, the game or social engagement or church, and helps the rest of the family to be ready also. To always be late is a sign of not caring for other people's feelings, in fact, it is selfish to always be late. So be on time, have your family ready, and help your husband. Now here again, you may have to train your husband. Be honest. Let him know you need his help in getting the little ones ready. Don't play the martyr role. Seek his help. But don't expect him to take care of everything.

Another area of concern for the housewife is in this business of watching television soap operas. I knew one woman who got so involved in the lives of the characters in "As the World Turns" that when one of the characters got sick, she asked us to pray for him during our prayer-meeting time. Now that is really getting confused as to what is real and what isn't! I had one lady tell me how much she was learning by watching these dramas. She said she was learning how to relate to people, yet she always managed to be in hot water with someone, her house was a mess and her own appearance left much to be desired. It's no wonder her marriage degenerated into a depressed state. I'm not saying that all television is bad—but I am saying that there is little to be learned from it to help us form a positive Christian life, and certainly countless hours are lost watching these soap operas. Take that time and bake a cake or some good homemade bread as an expression of love to your family.

Another area that makes a housewife beautiful is the control she has over her children. A Christian woman runs her household well. Teach your children by the example of your own life. If you are beautiful on the inside, so will your children be. And not only on the inside but beautiful on the outside as well.

I was visiting in a home a while ago, and it struck me that the wife was talking rather loudly. She would burst out laughing everytime she said something. I later discovered that she had never been able to say what she felt and so would try to impress others with her outward manner of laughing. Now there is nothing wrong with laughing, but when it is used to cover up true feelings of anger and anxiety or an inferiority complex, then it is dishonest.

A person who uses jesting and joking or is otherwise being showy, is usually trying to cover up some inner conflict or unresolved problem.

One really big danger in marriage is in this area of humor, jesting and teasing.

> Neither filthiness, nor foolish talking, nor jesting, which are not convenient; but rather giving of thanks (Ephesians 5:4 KJV).

Wives are prone to tease their husbands in public to get back at them. Women are also guilty, and men too, of trying to be "funny" or "cute" with cutting remarks. But cutting people down should have no place in a Christian's life. If you feel hurt or anger toward someone, be honest and confront them. You are being dishonest if you joke, and your jokes won't be harmless, they will really hurt.

There are a lot of instances when the woman will tease with another man, and in the process, feelings develop which lead to serious problems. "Picky, picky, picky" you think, but if you could see the heartache I have seen for just a little jesting, then you would heed these words; never tease, touch, or toy with other wives' husbands—if you do, you are way out of line.

If you find yourself always trying to be funny or making a joke out of situations that are not funny, then check your inner self, take an inventory. You probably will find that you are unhappy in your marriage, and you're trying to impress yourself and others that you are happy. Happiness is an inner joy that responds appropriately to each situation and does not necessarily mean going around with a silly grin. There is a lot to be said for good humor, but a lot of what we say is "put down" sarcasm and filth passed off as humor. When we take what is holy, the human body, and make all kinds of dirty jokes about it, then we are desecrating God's holy temple. We find ourselves laughing, when we should be angry. Many women will put up with dirty jokes and even participate in telling them. This shows weakness of character.

Another trait that the Christian woman has is that of confidence, and she gets her confidence from Christ. Now if you are having trouble making decisions and knowing what to do, if you feel confused, check out your mate. Perhaps he has been putting you down. Maybe he tells you that you can never do anything right. Let me tell you a secret about men. They usually feel that their wife is way out front. They see her ease, her self-assurance, her confidence. If they are insecure themselves and haven't matured, then they will pull her down. So help your husband up, and don't let him knock you down. Keep your confidence. Make a decision even if it is a wrong one. Then take the responsibility and learn from it.

For example, I once bought a small table from a junk shop. I took it to my neighbor, Mr. Tooke. As he was skilled in refinishing furniture, he helped me sand it down professionally with all his electrical tools. I was so proud of that little table. I refinished it and even felt more proud of it. I put it in the living room with a flower arrangement on top of it and some books on the lower shelf.

Several weeks later I was in my daughter's room and noticed she could use a nightstand by her bed. I immediately thought of the little table. Only one problem. Her bedroom suite is white French Provincial. Should I redo the little table or try to purchase another one? Since I couldn't afford another one, and the one I had was so perfect and petite, I wanted to use it. But I hesitated to redo it after all my work. A very wise person came by that day, and I told her about my dilemma. She told me to make a decision, even if it was a wrong one, but make the decision.

After she left, I went directly to the living room took the little table outside and immediately began painting it white to match Plythe's bedroom. To this day, the little table is by her bedside.

So go ahead and make the decision, whether it be right or wrong. Your confidence will grow and you'll be making more right decisions than wrong ones.

Some men feel threatened and are jealous because women are usually more intuitive and intellectual and common-sensed, or so they think. I know one couple who had agreed to plant a rose garden. The wife went to the library and checked out and read books on how to plant roses. The husband is a college graduate specializing in agriculture-horticulture. They set out to plant the rose bed. The wife suggested planting the roses according to the book. The husband got angry and said she didn't know anything about it. He said, "I have the degree, you don't." She gave in.

Weeks later, the roses weren't doing too well. The wife went out to check on them and found aphids all over them. She told her husband. He told her she didn't even know what an aphid was.

Not to be outdone, he went out and checked the roses and came in and said, "Well, they are dead aphids." He just wouldn't admit he had made a mistake.

Now this wife needs to keep up her confidence and bring her

husband up to her level, instead of letting him bring her down to his. She will have to continually confront him until he is honest with himself, and can accept the fact that she is right. She loves him and only wants to help him. Why should they compete?

One of the fruits of the Holy Spirit is kindness. This truly gives inner beauty. I can't think of anything more our marriages need these days than kindness and understanding. The godly woman will be kind to her spouse. And when you are in Christ, it is so much easier to respond kindly.

I remember one time our church was getting ready for Vacation Bible School. On Saturday afternoon, Page brought in several Bible School packets and asked our children, Perry and Plythe, then thirteen and eight, to put the handwork projects together so he could display them in Fellowship Hall the next day to announce Bible School's opening on Monday. I was busy cooking and cleaning, getting ready for Sunday. The children spent all afternoon in the den quietly working on the Bible School project.

After about three hours, Page came in, and I heard him fussing at the children. I walked in the den and, to my horror, there were pieces of handwork all over the room and not the first thing put together. Page was still fussing. I started reading the instructions and exclaimed, "Honey, no wonder the children couldn't put these together; I can't even understand them."

Page started picking up everything and mumbled he would do it himself. He took everything to the kitchen table. I would much rather he would have left everything in the den, but I didn't argue. I just motioned for the children to help daddy get everything to the kitchen table, and there we four sat for another three hours laughing and talking and putting the projects together.

Later that evening Page said, "Patti, you were beautiful this afternoon. I really appreciated your kindness. I was so angry when I came in, but you helped me switch gears by being so kind and thoughtful."

The "real me," without God's help, would have had a fit, having just cleaned house and then having two rooms all cluttered up. But it was a good feeling being kind.

I once heard a minister's wife give this testimony at a luncheon. She began with how sick she had been all her married life, and how she seemed to develop every illness that had a name and some that didn't. She was very ill mentally, as well, and she said her only two prayers were that she would die, and that before she did, a big Mack truck would run over her husband. I couldn't help but laugh to myself as I realized I had not prayed quite this way, but I could identify with her feelings.

She had lived with her husband twenty years and all through their marriage he had put himself, church, and then her in that order in his thinking. She responded by being angry. What she didn't realize, until things got so bad that she gave up to God, was that because of her anger, her husband could do nothing right in her sight. After realizing she was angry with her husband and confessing this to God, she began to try to help her husband in the areas where he needed it, in establishing priorities, seeking first God, and then her welfare, and then being concerned for the church. Her husband wasn't too sure about the change, but he, too, was at his wit's end with financial worries due to her illnesses. Noticing her change in attitude, he finally decided it couldn't do any harm. Praise God, they are now a living witness to God and His glory.

The point I am trying to make is that to have inner beauty, we need to know how to handle anger. The Bible says, be angry and sin not. I think Christ showed a healthy anger when He got rid of the money changers in the temple. He confronted them and was honest. Anger is a positive emotion, a demand "that you recognize my worth." But growing anger in a person can become unhealthy and can cut individuals off from each other if not handled properly.

You can be angry, but handle your anger quickly, confront the one with whom you are angry. Be loving and caring and respecting enough of your husband or others, not letting your feelings divide you.

Maybe your husband hurt your feelings two weeks ago and gave no apology. Maybe your neighbor or your best friend cut you down and gave no apology. Maybe your son didn't like the gift you gave him and didn't thank you for it, and you are feeling angry at everyone and everything. As I said, anger can be a demand. I demand you show me respect or appreciation.

A demand could also be a feeling. I feel my husband should do this or that. I feel my mother should be a babysitter for me; I feel the church choir isn't going right. You can ask yourself, "Are these feelings or demands clear? Are they legitimate? Shall I stick with them, or should I laugh at them and forget them? Start saying what you expect of others out loud, and if they are legitimate expectations, you can continue with them, and if they are not, you can cancel them. Many people are more hurt by what they expect and don't get from their friends than by what their friends actually do to them. If you are always silently expecting things from other people, you will often be hurt and disappointed as they may not always come through the way you want them to. Love is being honest and open about your demands and expectations. Love can cancel out unfair demands. Love is freeing others to live and grow.

Here is how Linda was able to cancel out an unfair demand she made on her husband. She and Joe had just moved into a new home out in the country where they had plenty of room. After three hectic days of moving and working hard all day and half the night, they were exhausted and had had very little communication.

Then Linda remembered at ten o'clock one night that she had forgotten to plant a few plants that she had dug up from the other house. She mentioned it to Joe, and he became angry because she wanted to go out and plant them. She wouldn't have time the next day, as she had to leave the house around 7 a.m. to go to work. Very reluctantly, Joe got a shovel and flashlight, and he and Linda tiptoed out into the darkness. They were no sooner out there shoveling away when they looked around and saw their two little children in pajamas and barefooted.

Joe looked at Linda and said, "Are you thinking what I am thinking?"

"What are you thinking?"

Joe said, "I'm thinking the neighbors must think we are crazy out here in the middle of the night shoveling with the whole family."

Linda said, still fairly angry, "They probably think we are burying a body." Joe howled with laughter, and though tired and weary, they hugged each other. Joe gave in to Linda's demand, and then Linda canceled out her anger with humor realizing that it wasn't a legitimate demand.

To have your husband say, "You are beautiful," and know he is talking about the inner you, is probably the sweetest compliment you will ever hear.

You don't have to be a doormat. How do you expect your husband to sweep you off your feet if he is standing on you? Remember to have that "inner beauty."

Seek ye first the kingdom of God, and his righteousness; and all these things shall be added unto you (Matthew 6:33 KJV).

Chapter 10

The Power of a Positive No

Women seem to find it difficult to say no. We wives need to help others since neighborliness is an important part of life, but that doesn't mean we can give all our time and attention to others to the exclusion of our family. Get your priorities straight. God first, family second, and then others.

We women have a bad habit of not being able to say no and then griping and complaining all the while we are doing the deed. I remember a lesson I learned the hard way. One day a friend called and asked if she could come by for a few minutes. Well, I really didn't have time to stop and visit with her as I was having a rather large dinner party that evening and I was busy cleaning house and cooking. However, I was unable to say no. She seemed to need me.

To my horror when I greeted her at the door, she had her little boy of four and her little girl of six months with her. I knew the little boy from past experience, and he was a terror. While my friend and I sat in the living room and talked, her little girl pulled all the grapes off the centerpiece on my glasstop table. She also had fingerprints all over the glass top and spots on it where she had burped up part of her bottle. As I was grinning on the outside to cover the seething on the inside, her little boy came indoors all wet from having gone swimming in my child's little pool. He ran through the house and jumped up on my kingsize bed and pulled down the covers getting everything all wet. The mother finally got up and spanked him. While she was spanking him, he tinkled all over the bedroom carpet, and since she jerked him up so quickly, his bubble gum flew out of his mouth and matted in the carpet.

A few weeks later, the friend called again. This time I not only said no but I confronted her with the situation. She thanked me for being honest, and after that, she would come by and visit from time to time without the children, or if she brought them, she would not let them out of her sight, and we were able to enjoy each other's company.

Women say yes many times just to win approval. They will do things with their husbands and grumble the whole time. Rather than being honest and letting your husband know you don't really enjoy the football games or you really don't like going to cow sales, you say yes and make the trip miserable for all. We do the same with the ladies at the church. We can't say no and end up baking all the pies and then seething and resenting everyone because nobody mentioned how good they were or how much they appreciated our doing it.

Many women feel guilty and therefore can't say no. One woman told me after she went back to work that she kept buying her teenage daughter everything she wanted, and the daughter was spoiled rotten. The mother knew in her heart she wasn't giving her daughter time and attention and thus couldn't say no to anything the girl wanted. She ended up with a selfish, spoiled child and guilty feelings on her part.

Also we try not to hurt anyone's feelings. Many times I have had ladies in the church ask me to go someplace, and because I didn't want to hurt their feelings, I would go, often at the expense of my family.

Also many times we can't say no because we want to protect our image. I think this was one thing I have had to work through as a pastor's wife. I always thought I had to set the example and never say no and always be willing to do everything, anytime. Had I kept up that pace, I wouldn't be here to write about it. Women do things because they are the boss's wife and the president's wife, etc., and feel that they have a certain image to keep up. But believe me, you will be much better off if you say no.

Beware of the woman who offers to do something for you and then says, "I'll let you do something for me sometime." Many times we can't say no because we feel if they ask us a favor, then we can expect a request in return. "I'll pick up your child this week, if you will get mine next."

Learn to say no if you really don't want to do it. Especially if it will make you feel resentful. When your motives are pure and your attitude is right, you need no excuse. Just say the truth.

We women are obligated to do things for our family, friends and community. We want to, it is a part of our make-up, even though social commitments limit our own freedom. Yet we want to sacrifice ourselves, as such involvement makes life so much richer and more meaningful. We must give, but not in order to get. We must be able to separate legitimate demands from those that are unreasonable. We must remember our first obligation is to God and to our family.

"Harriet, doggone it. You have lent me out again. I am so tired of you offering me for the school carnival. I have enough to do without you thinking something else up for me. You know those ladies are never satisified. After I put the booth up, they keep hounding me. Why do you do it? Just to make you look good. Just to be agreeable. At least you could ask me first," wailed Jim.

"Ann, I am sick and tired of you bringing home projects and spreading the mess all over the house. Worse yet, I can't stand this grumbling you are doing about the other girls. Now that you are committed to doing the project, do it and shut up. At least the other girls were smart. They aren't doing it, and their husbands don't have to put up with this complaining," yelled Bill.

Worse yet, is the Christian wife doing a project for the church and complaining about everyone else who didn't participate. Poor husband. What he has to put up with.

Check your motives for doing things. If you expect praise, you are doing them for the wrong motive. If you expect recognition, you are doing it for the wrong motive. If you do deeds for others because you want to, then praise the Lord.

Chapter 11

Leave and Cleave

Many young housewives today have the idea that their mother and father are always available. Sometimes the wife tends to lean more on her mother and father then she does on her husband.

Ladies, this can make your husband feel inferior. Now he may say it doesn't hurt his ego. Actually, he might even act like he enjoys their support, but if he were honest with himself and you, he would have to admit that it takes away from his manhood. So be aware of your husband's feelings. Don't be mom and dad's little girl—be your husband's wife.

Some young women have the mistaken idea that the grandparents are made for baby-sitting. Now I grant you, most grandparents enjoy this and welcome the grandchildren. But young people need to be sensitive to the grandparents and never take them for granted. Remember, if your children get on your nerves, and you are only twenty-five, think how they must get on mom's at fifty-five. Always be sure to ask the grandparents if they are going to be free for the evening. Then tell them exactly what you have in mind.

Many young couples actually get angry because the grandparents don't take an interest in their children as they feel they ought to. Don't take advantage of your parents, your neighbors, or your friends to watch your children. As a young couple, you do need to get away from the children once in a while, but take the responsibility to hire a baby-sitter. If you can't afford one, perhaps you can form a baby-sitting co-op or exchange service. If you happen to have parents who take care of your children once in a while and seem to enjoy it, then praise God, but don't take advantage of their generosity.

I hear so many grandmothers complain that they feel as though their daughters have taken advantage of them. Of course, I don't sympathize with the grandmother either because all she has to say is no. Maybe you are a young housewife with three small children all under the age of five. You're worn out and worn down. You need to get away from the kiddies. Talk with your husband and tell him you would like him to keep them on his afternoon off or one evening so you can go to a meeting. These children are his responsibility, too. Why do you think God gave children two parents? So when one got tired, the other could take over. Let your husband know exactly how you feel about being burdened down with all the responsibility. After all, they need time to be with their dad and learn to love him. Remember, love is built on relationships. If they never relate to their father, how can they love him? The same is true with the father; if he never relates to the baby and the little ones, how can he love them?

Don't let your husband make you feel guilty when you confront him with the idea of his taking care of the children for a while. He may have worked hard all day—so have you—but he still has a responsibility to his family. He needs to get down and romp and play with the children. I could cringe when I see some fathers push their children aside for a football game. I have even known some fathers who jokingly say: "Aw, go play on the freeway." This is not funny. Wives must see to it that they not only take their responsibility as wife and mother, but that they help the husband take his. Men can be stubborn in this area, so you will have to pray a lot.

One other area we have much to learn in is being honest in our relationship with our in-laws. The husband must realize that he is to protect the wife and not take sides against her. And the wife must do the same for her husband. No matter what your parents say about your husband, your loyalty is with him. You are one flesh—one in Christ.

Also, don't neglect your husband to enjoy the comforts of your family—your aunts, sisters, etc. I know one woman who neglected her immediate family, her son, daughter, and husband, to be with her sisters. Her sisters seemed more important to her. Remember your priorities; God first, and then your immediate family.

If you are out of order, putting others first before your own family, then you must go back and work out some psychological problems from your background that mixed your priorities in the first place.

I remember a friend who became a drug addict. She had a domineering mother, and, when she married, she could not cut the apron strings. Janet was forty-two-years-old and had teenagers, yet she still acted like a child because of her domineering mother. She ended up divorcing her husband, because she never took up for him when her mother put him down. Her mother was always finding fault with Janet's husband and Janet's children. The children grew up hating the grandmother, because she was always there and made their own mother look inferior. She was always putting Janet down. The children would see the grandmother coming and would giggle and say, "Here comes grandma on her broomstick."

Janet and her mother were parasites on each other. Janet could do nothing on her own, yet hated her mother and resented her for bringing her up so dependent on her. The mother was all alone and wanted Janet to be dependent so she wouldn't be alone in life. This is a sick, selfish situation. Janet could not face life and began burying herself in drugs. Her mother would not permit her to grow up. Janet's children, as a result, all had emotional problems.

Have healthy relationships with your family. Love them, but know your priorities.

Chapter 12

The End of The Tunnel

There is something I'd like to get into now that comes under the heading of "Protection." What happens to many wives is that they feel they are being forced into the masculine role. Please do not let this happen, although I realize that it is an ever-present temptation. Let me illustrate.

I watched this inverting of the masculine-feminine roles take place in a family near us. As her husband participated less and less in taking care of the finances, home, and business side of the marriage, his wife began taking over in these areas. She mowed the lawn, and when the house needed painting, or there were repairs that needed attention, she would end up being a carpenter, plumber, painter, and yardman. Then she started being a mechanic when the car did not work properly. She went to work to help supplement the income, because her husband was not managing the finances. Instead of helping him learn how to manage and to budget their money she went to work. Her salary was higher than her husband's and she found that she could actually be independent. She got her own checking account, her own insurance and her own car and finally woke up one morning and decided that she did not need her husband. He was a drag, a bore, and a stumbling block. She declared her independence, sued for divorce, and is now very unhappily unmarried.

What she did was wrong. She never should have started doing the yard work and the repair work around the house. She should have insisted that her husband do it. She never should have gone to work. She should have confronted her husband with his need to pay her more attention. What happened? She kept wanting to buy things, and her husband, because of his weakness and lack of love for his wife, could not refuse her, so she got them in debt up to their ears. She then went to work and found out she did not need a guy around who simply ate and slept, and actually contributed to the home trouble. On the other hand, he would not have been so obnoxious had she remained in her feminine role and insisted on her husband staying in his protective masculine role. It saps the life out of the family tree when the roles get inverted. Your job is to trust God to help you help your husband become the man God intended him to be.

There is a great danger in our country in these days with women becoming more masculine and men becoming more feminine. God intends that the two become one all right, but not by blending into neuter which equals nothing, nor by crisscrossing the sexes, but by the man being masculine and the woman being feminine.

It is true we need a better definition of masculinity and femininity but for God's sake, let's not allow what definitions we have get confused or inverted. This is perhaps the most insidious trick of Satan in the history of mankind to destroy the divine institution of marriage.

Women who revolt against their husbands' lack of protection by taking over are really on dangerous ground. When a woman declares her independence, she is making a gross error, for she is really revolting against God, and that is serious business. It may very well be that you can live without your husband and indeed do better. However, God has given you a job to do, so stop being selfish and get to it.

Now, what do you do? Look around. Open your eyes and try to see what it is you are doing that your husband should be doing. In each case, begin showing him, in a patient and loving way, how to do the job.

Woman is a responder not the aggressor.

> And Ruth said, Intreat me not to leave thee, or to return from following after thee: for whither thou goest, I will go; and where thou lodgest, I will lodge: thy people shall be my people, and thy God my God (Ruth 1:16 KJV).

This beautiful story of Ruth and Naomi shows a woman's devotion, the kind of devotion we need to have with our husbands. Ruth followed in God's divine order and went into the unknown, so to speak, because of her devotion. No matter what the circumstances were, she promised to follow. We women need to have this devotion and response to our husbands. Many times we do not fully understand what they want or which way things will turn out, but because of our faithfulness to our husbands and to God, we follow.

I know what some of you are thinking. What do I do when my husband isn't even a Christian? You respond to God's guidance in your life. You respond to His will for your life, and because you are seeking His will, He will show you how to lead your husband to salvation and divine order, not through overt aggressiveness, but through kindness and love and affection.

Most women don't want to be the aggressor. They want to come under submission. They want the husband to lead and be the head of the home and take responsibility. And things will happen when the woman really wants to respond. But she has to want to. She has to feel that urgent need to come under her husband. She has to be willing to be patient, loving, and kind, although her husband is slow to learn. The more love she displays in discipline, in truth, in thoughts and desires, the more the man learns. The more he learns, the more he matures and becomes acquainted with his responsibility. Then this responsibility feels good to him, and he is ready to take on more and more, until at last he becomes the head of the home.

One masculine role, according to the Bible, that women have virtually taken over is in the area of spiritual matters. This is out of line, for man is to be the spiritual leader—the prophet, priest, and king in his kingdom.

As the prophet, he represents God to his family; as a priest, he represents his family to God; as a king, he offers protection and provision for his little kingdom. If you have been guilty of taking over the business of spiritual matters in your family, then you need to begin now to change your attitude.

Women today are impatient with the progress and leadership of the men in our churches. We are way out of line. Many women use the church to fight their marital battles. If we don't feel the men are doing a good job in the church, we push them aside and take the attitude, "I'll do it myself," or "I'll show you." This is not being submissive.

Take the case of John and Mary. They have been married twenty years and have been faithful church workers, so faithful, in fact, they have been known to "run the church." Yet this couple can't communicate, their home is in disorder, and their children are unruly. They have not brought them up in Bible doctrine or set a Christian example for them even though they have been faithful to the church.

Because they can't communicate at home, they use the church as a way of staying together. This is how it goes. When Mary dislikes something at the church, she gripes and grumbles, not to the person to whom the complaint is rightfully due, but to her husband. He gets angry, blows up, and blows up the rest of the church with him. They usually get their way, and things do get done, not to the glory of God, but to the glory of Mary and John. They can list everything they ever did for the church.

Poor John has let Mary run all over him, and the only real authority he has is in the church. There he seems to feel safe in exploiting his feelings. Mary doesn't realize she is using the church to try to get John to take authority, and he does take it in the church but not at home. Why? John uses the church as a cop-out. He doesn't want to face facts and reality at home and take on the home responsibility, but he can manage the church when he gets hot-headed enough. For John, taking on the home is too much with his immature attitude.

Mary needs to realize that her hostility is not toward the church but toward John. The only place she can get him to take authority is in the church. This is out of line. She has to realize that they need to get their home in order. She needs to back off and give her devotion to John as unto the Lord so he can become the authority in their home.

> For if a man can't make his own little family behave, how can he help the whole church? (I Timothy 3:5 TLB).

The woman's role is a supportive role, and when a woman begins to over-assert herself in the home or church, she is out of God's order.

If you love your husband, you will be loyal to him no matter what the cost. You will always believe in him, always expect the best of him, and always stand your ground in defending him. It is your job to help your husband take on more responsibility, not less. It is your job to guide him into a deeper understanding of his role in the family. This is a lifetime job, so don't ever think that you've got it made—there is an infinite amount of truth for couples to discover together, to learn from each other, to share with their children. Each phase of life brings added responsibilities and fresh insights into family living. There is such a vast frontier before us, we need never feel that we've discovered it all.

> Her children stand and bless her; so does her husband. He praises her with these words: "There are many fine women in the world, but you are the best of them all!" (Proverbs 31:28-29 TLB).

Praise the Lord!